Two Weeks and 4,100 miles
with the Women's Freedom Ride

PAULA O'KRAY

www.ten16press.com - Waukesha, WI

Kickstands Up!:
Two Weeks and 4,100 miles with the Women's Freedom Ride
Copyrighted © 2019 Paula O'Kray
ISBN 978-1-64538-029-0
Second Edition

Kickstands Up!:
Two Weeks and 4,100 miles with the Women's Freedom Ride
by Paula O'Kray

All Rights Reserved. Written permission must be secured from the publisher to use or reproduce any part of this book, except for brief quotations in critical reviews or articles.

For information, please contact:

www.ten16press.com
Waukesha, WI

Cover photography by Mark Vicker
Photo credits (unless otherwise indicated): Paula O'Kray

The author has made every effort to ensure that the information within this book was accurate at the time of publication. The author does not assume and hereby disclaims any liability to any party for any loss, damage, or disruption caused by errors or omissions, whether such errors or omissions result from accident, negligence, or any other cause.

This book is dedicated to Karen "Momma Bear" Collins and the women of the Women's Freedom Ride.

Table of Contents

Acknowledgments iv
The Idea 3
The Search for Adventure 5
Dreaming Bigger 14
The Dream Becomes Reality 16
  Mid-February
  Last week of February
  Saturday, February 25
Getting from Point A to Point B 22
  Mid-March
Packing Practice 30
  First Weekend in April: 62 Days to Kickstands Up!
The Preparations Continue 38
The Other Side of the Ride 40
Final Preparations 42
  April 13: 46 Days to Kickstands Up!
  First Week of May: 35 Days to Kickstands Up!
  Third Week of May: 18 Days to Kickstands Up!
The Grand Adventure Begins! 54
0 to 85 mph in 24 Hours, or …
It's Not a Learning Curve, It's a Cliff! 62
  Monday, June 5: Paducah, Kentucky, to Blue Springs, Missouri
Biker Girl Meltdowns and Racing against the Storm 91
  Tuesday, June 6: Blue Springs, Missouri, to Hays, Kansas

A New Perspective on Traffic, Mountains, and Wind 99
   Wednesday, June 7: Hays, Kansas, to Fort Collins, Colorado
So, Who Are the Women
of the Women's Freedom Ride? 103
   Thursday, June 8: Fort Collins, Colorado, to Rock Springs, Wyoming
Commandeering the Local IHOP,
Bike Drops at Gas Stops, and a Day Off 111
   Friday, June 9: Rock Springs, Wyoming, to Idaho Falls, Idaho
Cold Mornings, Bad Hotels,
and a Very Special Dinner Guest 120
   Sunday, June 11: Idaho Falls, Idaho, to Billings, Montana
   Monday, June 12: Billings, Montana, to Deadwood, South Dakota
A Day Off in Deadwood and
a Very Long Day in South Dakota 128
   Tuesday, June 13: A Layover Day in Deadwood, South Dakota
   Wednesday, June 14: Deadwood, South Dakota, to Fairmont, Minnesota
Back to Wisconsin, Bike Night in Milwaukee,
and Saying Goodbye 137
   Thursday, June 15: Fairmont, Minnesota, to Milwaukee, Wisconsin
   Saturday, June 17: Last Day of My Ride
Epilogue: All Good Things Must Come to an End…
or Must They? 146

Appendix: Bike Stats 149
Appendix: GoFundMe Letter 150
Appendix: Packing Suggestions 152
Appendix: Women's Freedom Ride 2017
Stops at a Glance 160
More from Paula 161

Acknowledgments

I would like to sincerely thank everyone who helped me prepare for this ride, in every possible way. From those who encouraged me with words, donations, or items for the trip, given or borrowed; to those who helped with their professional skills, making sure my body would be able to handle the physicality of the ride, in particular Dr. Dean, my chiropractor; and Brian, my massage therapist.

I also want to give a shout-out to the great guys in the service department at Donahue Super Sports, who did a thorough check on the bike to make sure it would handle all those miles; and the amazing guys at Wilshire Trailers for updating the bike with all the modifications I requested and making sure I'd be comfy for all those miles. You rock!

Thanks also to those people "behind the scenes" who kept things going at home: my friend Larry, for checking on the house and calming me down when the big storm hit; Karen, who took good care of my pup and spoiled her while I was away; and above all, my co-worker Amy, who covered for me at the paper during those two weeks I was gone. You are a saint!

But most of all, thanks to all the fans and readers of my column. Thanks for being a part of my adventure. I wasn't sure what to expect when I began, but it turned into quite a wonderful odyssey, and I couldn't have done it without your hopes, prayers, and support. It means a lot to me. So thank you for that, from the bottom of my heart.

Deep thanks to Carolyn my editor for making me a better writer, as well as Lauren and Shannon at TEN16 Press for their support, guidance and patience. Writing this book had been a great experience and I'm already looking forward to the next one!

Thanks also to Ginny Davis Bigback for her great ideas, suggestions, and the test shots for the book cover, and Mark Vicker for the final cover photography. The fickle Wisconsin weather certainly made it a challenge in both cases, and I appreciate your talent and enthusiasm.

I was surprised at the diversity of people this story appealed to, and I'd like to thank everyone who encouraged me to put it into a book. There are far too many of you to mention - in fact, many of you were strangers in passing, and I don't know your names. Be assured though, that your words of support were deeply appreciated and made me feel amazing. I hope you enjoy this book as much as I enjoyed putting it together for you, and I hope it encourages you to get out there and live the life you imagine.

Kick Stands Up!

Two Weeks and 4,100 miles
with the Women's Freedom Ride

The Idea

I'm not sure exactly when I got the idea to do the Women's Freedom Ride. In general, I had been looking for adventurous things to do for quite awhile. I'd written a weekly column since 2012 for the newspaper I worked for, and, over the years, I'd gotten a lot of positive feedback on it. The column was generally musings about my perspective from the middle of life, hence the title "Middle of the Road." It was an homage to the song by The Pretenders, about the same topic.

The editor of the paper pretty much let me write about whatever I wanted. I tried to keep the columns as positive and entertaining as I could, but they were sometimes serious, poignant, or a not-so-thinly-veiled, all-out rant. The stories reflected the day-to-day reality of life. Thankfully, the majority of the feedback by far was very positive and supportive. But mostly what I heard from a lot of people, especially women, is how brave I am.

I don't know that I'm really that brave. I think it's more that I just don't know when to quit. Plus, I don't like hearing the word "no" or "can't." And sometimes that's a good thing. So as this feedback kept coming in, I started to realize that what I do and say is an inspiration to a lot of people out there who are just watching life, and not participating in it the way they should be. I used to be one of those people.

I used to think doing big, exciting things was just for a certain kind of person. But one day it struck me that we work our jobs all day (or night) long, and we come home and watch other people living their lives on television. We watch others doing things we could be doing. And the absurdity of that thought is what motivated me to start living my life differently.

So I did. I stopped watching television. I canceled my cable subscription. I tried to identify the things that kept me from doing the things I really wanted to do, and then I minimized those as much as I could. I tried to identify the things that really made me happy, made me feel fulfilled. I maximized those as much as I could. I found myself finding ways to spend more time outside, with my dog, in my kayak, and on my motorcycle.

Even then, when I was immersed in these activities, I found myself approached by women who kept telling me how brave I was. Still, I did not exactly feel brave. Was I brave? I started with small, simple things and gradually built up to bigger things. That seems to be how it happened for me. When you open a door to a new room, new things start to happen.

The Search for Adventure

When you start having adventures, it's like eating potato chips—it's hard to have just one. Over the years I found myself amping up my adventures without really trying. Over a decade ago, when I was still married, I signed up for a four-day artist's retreat in Mineral Point, Wisconsin, attending alone without knowing a soul. It was like stepping off a cliff for me, it was so intimidating. Ten minutes into the introduction by the lead speaker, I knew I was in the right place and had found my tribe. It was a gathering of creative people who loved the outdoors, and could recognize how art and natural materials could be brought together to create objects with deep, significant meaning, and help others find a connection to nature. They spoke in phrases that were familiar to me, and it was clear they put a great value on this connection, and supported each other's ideas without judgment. It was a "yes we can" environment when in the real world creatives are very familiar with "no you can't" responses. I was validated and empowered in that moment, and wanted to immerse myself in that atmosphere. I met many wonderful people that year, and returned for many years to "recharge" my creative batteries annually. I still occasionally attend this creative summer weekend retreat at Shake Rag Alley, and quite a few of those acquaintances are dear friends now, simply because I made a brave decision to strike out and try something new on my own.

Community theater was the same sort of adventure. I found theater about the same time my marriage was falling apart, and losing myself in it proved to be great therapy for me. I became involved in many aspects of producing a show with a diverse group of volunteers. Those people became like family to me over the years, and still are. There is no comparison to the teamwork of putting on a great show for the community.

It was at this point I started looking for adventures to go on. I had been bitten by the bug, and began actively seeking out neat experiences to write about in my column.

I decided to participate in a four-day sea kayak symposium in Munising, Michigan, with friends I had made in a local kayak group in my town. Four days on Lake Superior learning about paddles, padding and how kayaks move through big water, not to mention some very long portages and a few impromptu rescue exercises made my hips feel like falling off, but also formed new and greater bonds of friendship. I really had a grand time pushing my boundaries, learning new skills and building my self-confidence while getting to know the ladies of the group better, some of whom had been complete strangers on day one of the event.

For a winter adventure, I chose a three-day Becoming an Outdoors-Woman weekend in northern Wisconsin learning how to dogsled, skijor, and snowshoe.

For those unfamiliar, skijoring is a recreational activity where the skier is pulled along over the snow or ice by a horse, dog or motor vehicle, on relatively level ground. It's derived from the Norwegian word skikjøring, meaning ski driving. The skier wears a harness that encircles their hip area that is attached to a length of tow rope, and leans back into it as the dog (in this case) pulls the skier along. The skier uses the same terms to direct the dog (or dogs) for direction and speed as she would for dogsledding. "Gee" for right turns, "Haw" for left turns, "Line Out" to move the dog or dogs ahead until the line is taut before heading out, and "Hike" for "Let's go!"

It was an amazing weekend of empowering skill-building with nine other ladies and an amazing staff of instructors. So amazing, in fact, that it became a three-part column, there was so much to write about.

Besides the outstandingly delicious organic meals we were served three times a day in our hosts' home, there were the amazing sled dogs, each with a memorable personality. We learned about the parts of a dog sled and how it all works, and the terms needed to control a dog team out on the trails. The ladies cheered each other on as one by one, each returned successfully from her first attempts at being a musher. We also had the opportunity that weekend to cross-country ski and snowshoe through the glistening snow-filled woods surrounding the property. The ladies came from all walks of life, which led to some very interesting discussions around the dinner table . . . and that was just the first day!

The second day of the event, evaluated by confidence and skill, mushers were matched up to dog teams accordingly and given two rules, 1) Hold on, and 2) Don't let go. The chase team followed each musher down the trail in case something went

Clearly with these experiences, a pattern had been formed, and with increasing frequency. And now a new adventure had appeared on the horizon.

wrong, and things did. Of course, we learned many things from each returning musher, no matter how their run went. From face plants in the snow to making snow angels to tangled dogs and a crashed sled, there was no lack of fun and adventure that weekend. It was an amazing time that I would gladly do again. Learning something new with a group of amazing women is something everyone should experience.

Clearly with these experiences, a pattern had been formed, and with increasing frequency. And now a new adventure had appeared on the horizon.

But I'm getting ahead of myself. Before we talk about that adventure, you probably want to hear about how I came to be interested in motorcycles in the first place.

I grew up in the '60s, and motorcycles weren't a big part of my life. My sister owned a little, white Suzuki scooter, which was fun. My dad would take me on a ride on it once in a while. We also had a friend of the family who visited once in a great while on a Honda Gold Wing motorcycle, and he would take me on little rides and sometimes drop me off at school. It wasn't like we owned bikes or rode or raced them. I just thought they were neat. However, when I was old enough to get a bike, my dad wasn't happy about it. He told me that I would forget where the gas and the brake were and get myself in an accident, or worse. I wasn't happy that my dad had such little confidence in my skills, but it made me even more determined to find a bike and learn how to ride it properly.

I first purchased a motorcycle when I was in my early 20s, a 450 Kawasaki I bought from a friend's husband. Even though I took a course, I was never that comfortable or confident on it, and never got my license. I had failed the test, and was so angry about it that I vowed to drive on my temporary license forever. Did I mention that I'm a tad stubborn? Just a tad.

When I got married in my late 20s, I had to be more practical about life, and the bike went away. After all, you really can't get groceries for a family of four on a motorcycle.

Roughly 23 years later, after building a career in graphic design and raising a family, the end of my marriage was near. I took the course again, passing the test this time, and bought a new 950 Yamaha V-Star. The year was 2010.

I hadn't planned to buy a bike quite so big. When I went to the dealership, the sales rep happened to be a past co-worker of mine. He took me to the front of the store and asked me to try sitting on the bike in the window. It looked absolutely huge, and especially so because it was white. As I sat on the bike with a dubious look on my face, the sales rep told me, "You can handle this, Paula."

I replied, "You say that to all the girls. You just want to sell the bike." Then he offered me a test ride on an identical bike they had in the back, and I said, "Sure!"

The bike still seemed way too big for me, and after straddling it, I wasn't sure a test ride was such a good idea. But as soon as I rode away, it felt perfect, and I knew it was the bike for me. He was right—I could totally handle this bike!

I named her Xena.

Xena and I went on many adventures together, but always alone. I found that trying to find people to ride with as a single woman was practically impossible. I friended and followed dozens of women's riding pages on Facebook, but made very few, if any, contacts. I had gone on a few poker run charity rides in my area as well. Poker Runs are generally fund-raiser rides that invite a large group of riders to form a poker hand by stopping at several taverns in several counties and choosing a card at every stop. The cards are recorded, and the rider with the best "poker hand" wins a prize at the end of the ride. After the ride, there is usually a free meal, socialization among the riders, and a raffle of other door prizes.

I was generally considered a pariah on these rides, as Harley-Davidsons are quite popular when you live in the state where they're made, and I ride a Yamaha, or "rice-burner" as some have called it. Harley riders can be snobby, and I was generally ignored on these rides because I rode something else. I couldn't even get a road salute from Harley riders as we passed each other.

Going through a divorce, I developed such a profound sense of loss that I stopped feeling like material things were of any value whatsoever. Fighting over such trivial things seemed pointless.

In motorcycle culture, the road salute or "wave" is a general greeting given to other riders as you pass each other, honoring the kinship within the riding community. The salute can really be any sort of acknowledgment, a hand wave or sometimes just a simple nod, especially if your hands are busy shifting or braking. The hand can be open and up or out, but most often is two fingers pointed at a downward angle to the road. It's to indicate to "keep the rubber side down," or to keep your two tires on the road, and be safe. It's meant to be a friendly sign, but many times it's used to snub other riders for various reasons by denying them a salute as they pass. Best not to think too hard about it, and just "ride your own ride."

I also got used to random catcalls from strangers at stoplights, but I did notice the ladies riding on the backs of those bikes looking over at my ride with envious glares. "That's right, ladies," I thought, "I ride my own!"

Several years went by. I never considered selling my Xena, as she brought me great freedom and a feeling of independence. In fact, I would tell people that if my home ever caught fire, I would only need to save her and the dog. Nothing else really mattered. Going through a divorce, I developed such a profound sense of loss that I stopped feeling like material things were of any value whatsoever. Fighting over such trivial things seemed pointless. If I valued something, it was used for leverage and control, so I stopped valuing everything and resigned myself to the feeling that it would eventually all be taken away. I got to the point where I just wanted to be free and not have to dicker about what was mine or not mine. I stopped caring about what I got to keep. None of it mattered anymore.

I went on rides by myself. I found a few routes in and around my town that were just the right length and made me happy, and every once in awhile, I would string them all together for a long ride. I didn't go far from home, since I had no back-up, and if I got into trouble, I was the one I'd have to rely on to get myself out of it. It was always difficult to find friends available to ride with. I joined several riding groups on Facebook in hopes that I would eventually connect with women who lived fairly close to my area. Again, several years went by with few results.

Eventually I connected with Erika, a woman from a town about 45 miles north of mine in a group called Stilettos on Steel, and she began inviting me to local rides. As luck would have it, though, I couldn't make a lot of them, either for scheduling reasons or simply bad weather. We kept at it, though, and eventually met up to attend a Ladies' Bike Show in Bonduel, Wisconsin, several hours from my home.

I met Erika and a few other Stilettos at a gas station in a town about 30 miles north of my home. I wasn't sure how to act, since I had never really interacted with other women riders. Not in the 'real world' outside of Facebook, anyway. I didn't feel very confident and was worried it would show. Was I intimidated? Hell, yes! Was I about to let them know? Hell no.

Introductions were made, and polite conversation followed. I just tried to blend in, relax and go with the flow as best I could. Once we got on the highway though, Katie, the lead rider, took off at almost 80 miles an hour and never looked back, and the rest of the ladies followed suit. I was a bit freaked out, yet excited at the same time. I had to keep up, I was with the big dogs now! "It's now or never," I silently told myself as I hit the throttle, hard.

Once at the show, I was pleased and amazed at the variety and number of both bikes and women in attendance. I was introduced to and connected with a whole new community of interesting women who made me feel very warm and welcome from the very start. They were all very interested to know my story and how I had come to be a lady motorcyclist.

Later that afternoon, after the bike show had ended, the group took a nice long ride on the way back on backroads to enjoy the fall colors. It had been a big day for me, and by the end of the ride, I was really feeling it. The cold and the excitement of the day were kicking my ass, but I was pleased the day had gone so well. I was already looking forward to seeing the girls again sometime. It made me realize that all my homework was finally paying off.

When it came to motorcycling, I had noticed many rides around the country offering adventures for women who ride motorcycles. I often watched videos and read blogs about women who have traveled all over the world on their bikes, in many different capacities, and wondered if I would ever get the opportunity. The thought of riding my Yamaha 950 V-Star across the country sounded great, but I had no experience with such things. I had so many questions about where to begin.

Not long after that is when I heard about the Women's Freedom Ride. I learned it was an annual cross-country ride, held the first two weeks of June, that would be coming through Wisconsin.

The Women's Freedom Ride was started in 2013 to promote fellowship and support for all women riders, and also to raise money for a track wheelchair for a severely wounded veteran. That year, 13 riders rode from Charleston, South Carolina, to San Diego, California. In 2016, 23 women rode more than 5,500 miles, joined by hundreds of others over the course of 18 days in 18 states, to help the Military Warriors Support Foundation in providing a mortgage-free home for a wounded combat veteran and Purple Heart recipient.

The ride I planned to participate in had more than 43 registered riders who would be joined by many others as they traveled through 19 states in 18 days, riding more than 6,000 miles to raise funds to provide training for service dogs for disabled vets. The goal was $21,000, and 100 percent of the funds were to be given to the charity. Each rider covers her own expenses on the ride, and I was hoping to be one of them.

Dreaming Bigger

I took a look at all the ways I could make the trip work. Since I live in central Wisconsin, I decided to join the group from their stop in Fairmont, Minnesota, and ride with them to Milwaukee, Wisconsin—two full days of riding alone, one full day of riding with the group. I sent in my registration and check for the fee, and felt pretty proud of myself. I was going to be a part of the ride!

I let the Stiletto girls know what I had planned to do, hoping one or two might join me, but they were busy with life, and found it difficult to make it happen. I told them that was fine, that I was still going to do it. I had made up my mind. They were pretty excited for me, and sent lots of words of encouragement.

A few weeks went by, and during those days, I had a nagging thought. I looked at the paperwork I had done and thought, "What if?" What if money was no object? What if time was no object? What if there was nothing holding me back? What would it take to do the entire ride?

I sat down and started making serious plans. I looked at all the stops for the full ride, running 19 days from early to mid-June. I printed out a map and marked out the route, noting the length of riding between stops and the country it would wind through. The ride started in Charleston, South Carolina, headed west, looped through Colorado, Wyoming, and Idaho, and headed back through the northern states, turning south the last few days, and ending in North Carolina. I had always wanted to take a ride like this, I thought, but could never do it on my own. I didn't have the know-how, the experience, or the back-up staff to safely take it on, and that would take years to accumulate even if I attempted it. I quickly realized that I had to find a way to make it work, to make as many days as I could on the ride.

The Dream Becomes Reality

I figured if I drove directly south from Wisconsin, I could meet up with the group at their stop in Paducah, Kentucky. I would have to start two days early and spend the night in central Illinois, riding two full days on my own. That in itself would be an adventure, but I was willing to go for it. If I joined the group in Paducah, I could then ride with them for 16 days, looping out to the west through Kansas, north through Colorado and Idaho, and back through the northern states. I could leave the ride in Milwaukee when they left for Indiana. It seemed doable, so I decided to make it a reality.

Mid-February

After sending in my registration and fees, I was allowed to join a private Facebook group that showed the specific cities we would be stopping in and the hotel information. The page also allowed participants to find roommates and get to know each other a bit before the ride. It was only mid-February, but the ladies were excited, many sharing packing tips with those of use who were new to the whole experience. I started taking notes and quickly realized there was much more preparation than I had originally considered.

Beyond what to take, I had to think about my endurance

level for such a ride. I didn't want to hold the group back or be considered a liability. Other rides I had seen around the country had minimum experience requirements, which made me ask if our ride had any. Having spent four days in a kayak and having my back and hips start rebelling after a day and a half, I knew I had to make sure my body could handle being in the elements 300 to 500 miles a day for 16 days straight.

Karen Collins is the woman who started the Women's Freedom Ride, and she is an amazing, caring lady who never stops. Her nickname is "Momma Bear," because she makes sure everyone is taken care of, safe, and she's highly protective.

Karen has a great sense of responsibility for the participants of the ride. In the weeks leading up to the ride, she reminds everyone to take test rides on fully packed bikes and also to have their bikes checked over at the local shop. The tires, brakes, and everything else need to be in good shape to endure the long hours on the road, and to make sure every rider is riding safely.

During the ride, Momma Bear is up early to visually inspect the bikes, making sure no one has low air in her tires, and that all packs are mounted safely and securely on the bike. With all the weather, wind, and vibration from many miles on an interstate, an improperly secured load or loose equipment can be an accident waiting to happen. Momma also makes sure the group reviews the rules of the road before the ride begins in the morning, to make sure all the riders know the hand signals that keep the group rolling down the road safely.

It's team effort and awareness that keeps each and every woman safe, and Momma never misses an opportunity to improve the safety of the ride. In fact, when traffic allows, she'll fall back alongside the group while on the road to check in with each and every rider, to make sure they're doing all right. Giving Momma a thumbs-up, blowing her a kiss, or sticking your tongue out usually means you're good and happy. A thumbs-down or similar sign means there's a concern to address, and that's taken care of immediately. It's a great feeling to know you're in such good hands, and it adds a lot to the enjoyment of the ride.

Karen was very available to me and assured me there was no minimum experience level for the ride, but listed things that were necessities, like a license, bike registration, and proof of insurance. She also said to let her know if any other questions came up.

Meanwhile, I wrote out all the stops, and drew up a chart with the mileage between each, and the cost of the room for the night. I figured out my gas mileage, and the cost of lodging, fuel, and meals. The hardest thing, I thought, was how would I record my thoughts as we were hurtling down the interstate at 80 mph? I don't always recall with great accuracy the minute things that make a story worth telling, and rely on pen and paper for quite a lot of it. I wasn't going to have that luxury on this trip.

A camera, I thought, was the best way, since a photo can help you remember quite a bit about a moment. If I could figure out a way to have one strapped to my chest and just tap it when needed, that would be perfect. As I was discussing this with Joey, a co-worker of mine, she suggested a Go-Pro camera, and told me I could use hers if needed. That way I could speak my thoughts out loud, and the camera would pick it up for reference later. I came to understand that quite a few ladies on the ride mounted these cameras to their helmets.

A Go Pro is a compact camera capable of capturing photos and video in extreme conditions. The camera has a rugged frame that's smaller, and it's waterproof and virtually indestructible. These cameras can be mounted to a set of handlebars or a motorcycle helmet with a variety of mounting systems that are available.

Another interesting thing I noticed was the suggestion of wicking clothing. The ride doesn't stop for rain, so wicking is important. I found many of the suggestions for staying dry similar to the clothing that had been suggested for my kayaking adventure. Great, I thought, less to buy. There were also a lot of tips for how to pack in wet weather, like using two-gallon Ziploc bags for a day's worth of clothing, where the air could be easily pressed out to make the bag smaller for packing. Another great idea was to line the inside of a duffel bag with a large, plastic merchandise bag from a local store; that way the wind wouldn't be rattling it throughout the ride, and items inside would still stay dry.

Last week of February

Gary, my manager, a Harley guy from way back, donated a gel seat to the cause after hearing about my endeavor and a long discussion about "monkey butt," an affliction suffered by many long-range cyclists.

"My wife really enjoyed the gel seat for a long time until I upgraded to a better seat. It should work really well for you too."

There's also a powder called "Anti Monkey Butt" made to keep that area moisture free and thus unchafed, but I also wanted something to ease my butt bones after several hours in the saddle. Yes, I know . . . feel free to insert your favorite butt joke here. I had been considering an Air Hawk, an inflated seat that had come highly recommended, but considering how pricey the item is, I settled for the free gel seat. Gary had been to Sturgis on his bike many times, and also offered me a copy of his trip list, which was extremely helpful.

The Sturgis Motorcycle Rally is an American motorcycle rally held annually in Sturgis, South Dakota, for ten days, usually during the first full week of August. It was begun in 1938 by a group of Indian Motorcycle riders and was originally held for stunts and races. Attendance has historically been around 500,000 people, reaching a high of over 700,000 in 2015. For a lot of motorcyclists, it's the "must attend" event of the summer.

Great suggestions continued to roll in: CamelBaks for hydration, bungee nets to secure the load, packing practice runs, exercises for stomach and back strength, and loaded runs on the bike to build up stamina.

A CamelBak is a hydration system originally developed by the military to be worn as a backpack. A hose and a self-sealing mouthpiece extends from the pack and clips to the front of the straps, allowing the wearer to drink easily when biking, hiking, or, in this case, while riding for many miles without stopping.

I had trained for a day-long walking event called Walk Wisconsin in my state before, and training had always begun in mid-February. I was beginning to see a lot of similarities, and began to think about the ride in this way. Unfortunately, a beautiful, spring-like weekend was followed by six to ten inches of the white stuff at the end of the month, and practice runs had to be put on hold for a few more weeks.

Saturday, February 25

Time to find a roommate. I noticed a lot of people were chatting about finding roommates on the ride page, so I jumped in and started making inquiries. It didn't take long to find Christine, a rider from South Carolina, who was also looking. We split up the rooms by price, so each could make reservations for half the ride. However, later that same day, Diane, another rider from South Carolina, suggested we both to stay with her and her roommate for the trip, so the price could then be split by the four of us. Now that I had just found three buddies to room with, the trip was beginning to get interesting and exciting.

We became friends and private messaged about our bikes and levels of experience. I was a newbie, but all I found was a lot of support and encouragement. It was great, and I was looking forward to learning more about my new friends in the coming weeks.

Getting from Point A to Point B

Being a writer and wanting to expand my career in that direction as a women's adventure writer, I had been thinking for almost a year how to go about that. I had been keeping a binder full of ideas of all sorts of ways to do it, but hadn't really gotten very organized. Finally, when 2017 hit, I felt it was time to seriously move ahead with the project. I signed up for an online course about writing for internet markets to learn all I could about the best way to proceed. Meanwhile, I started thinking about who among the businesses I network with might be a potential sponsor or two. If I could get part of my trip paid for, that would be amazing, not to mention perhaps a few bucks for the charity we were raising money for.

I contacted a site I had been a featured blogger for, for many years. I had spent a lot of time on the site during my divorce looking for guidance and support, and through those efforts was offered the opportunity to write as a featured writer. After the pain of my divorce was in the past, I continued to write and offer other women going through the same experience the same guidance and support that I had received. I contacted Beth, the woman who had been my go-to person whenever I had a question, and she seemed excited about the idea. She needed more details before taking my idea to the powers that be, so we discussed what a sponsorship might look like. Armed with our ideas, she made the pitch, and . . . it was a no go. They wished me very well but couldn't offer me a sponsorship at the time. I took it as a learning experience and moved on.

I considered talking to the dealership where I had purchased the bike. I could write about the trip leading up to the big day, and then blog about it as I was on the road, posting to their website for other patrons to follow and enjoy. I thought they might even give me a break on the price for the highway bars I was going to need for the ride, as I realized that comfort was going to be an important aspect of my endurance.

Highway, or "crash," bars are loops of chrome-plated tubing mounted to each side of the motorcycle's lower frame near the front of the engine. They're designed to minimize damage to the bike if it falls on its side, protecting the engine and body panels. The bars stick out a few inches wider than the bike and are made in many different styles.

If nothing else, I would hit them up for a donation toward our cause. In the process, a friend suggested another dealership in the area that might be interested, a mom-and-pop cycle shop in a nearby town. I started making a list of who I was planning to talk to, and what I would say to them.

Of course, I didn't forget the newspaper I worked for. I hoped they would want to support me on the trip, since obviously I'd be writing my column about the trip, and my readers might enjoy participating by reading along and/or donating toward the cause. Finally, I considered generating a GoFundMe page to help with donations, giving people an easy way to put their money toward the cause if they so desired. Quite a lot to think about, and I spent many hours working toward my goals. Thankfully my dog, who's half Lab and half Chow and a beautiful shade of orange, would interrupt from time to time, as she will do, when I spend too much time at a glowing screen. Dog walks do wonders for the soul.

> *Google can show you pictures, but asking riders what they use and whether they would recommend something is gold.*

That, too, would need to be addressed: dog care for half a month. I have a dear friend, a past co-worker, who loves dogs as much as I do, and she and her husband will kidnap my dog on occasion when I am too busy to get to her. As a single person, this happens now and then, and I'm thankful for all the help I get. So one of the first questions I asked in mid-February was about finding good care for my pup of 11 years. Fortunately, my friend and her mom really enjoyed sharing my pup during the weekend I was gone for my dog sledding adventure, so they were both happy and willing to take her again. That was actually probably the biggest piece of the puzzle to solve for me, since there is no way I would want to board her for that long. I would have scrapped the trip at that point. Yes, she's that important to me.

I have to admit, I don't like to exercise. I walk daily with the dog, but it's really more of a stroll with lots of stops. So I had to start with sit-ups, push-ups, and planking, and I was really lukewarm about it. But I did it, and made notes each night to see my progress, so I would be encouraged to continue. Still, it was like mixing cement. I did miss a few days here and there, but I figured something was definitely better than nothing. I knew there was Ibuprofen to rescue me, but I also knew that if I had a strong core, the ride would be that much easier.

Mid-March

I spent the week asking questions on the ride's Facebook site. I already had a checklist from a co-worker who'd been to Sturgis many times, but I wanted to see what the ladies' lists looked like for comparison, so I asked. So many great suggestions, from basic things like bandannas for dust to tie-downs for gear, but it was a bit overwhelming. I decided to organize a list of things that I'd need the most and go about acquiring those first; then if there was time (and money) left to get a few luxuries, I would consider those.

Time to shop! I don't think I'd been this excited about a shopping spree since I went out to purchase my own tool bag and tools. I had taken rustic furniture classes for a few years and decided it was time, and what fun it was to choose my very own hammer, screwdrivers, and power drill! I have never regretted it.

I headed out one Saturday with a list of items and a lot of questions. Google can show you pictures, but asking riders what they use and whether they would recommend something is gold. I went to a shop about an hour from my home, since motorcycle shops are basically nonexistent in my own community.

It was a nice bike shop for such a small town. I asked a few questions and then decided to just look around on my own. I perused throttle stops, crash bars, face masks, cargo net bungees, fingerless gloves, bike covers, fitted leather vests, and rain gear.

Throttle stops are small pads that allow you to hold the throttle at one speed with the pad of your hand without actually gripping the throttle. It's a nice change and gives your hand a rest when needed, and is relatively inexpensive. The ladies of the ride had warned me not to install cruise control, since speeds change often and quickly on the ride, and you need to stay alert and responsive to these changes.

It was still a bit overwhelming, but I was beginning to get a sense of what I really needed and the amount of money I was looking at for all the gear. Budget was going to play a very large part in my choices.

It was amazing to see all the different ways there were to solve a problem on a motorcycle, not to mention all the ways to make it yours, and to stand out. I heard the sirens calling to me for a few moments, and then pulled myself back to reality. "Focus Paula," I said to myself.

I took note of the things I was interested in and their prices. Then I went back to the sales staff to ask my final questions. I needed highway pegs for comfort, but didn't really like the look of crash bars.

Highway pegs are foot rests that riders install on their bikes to give them alternatives for foot placement on long rides. This helps a great deal with comfort on the bike, as many hours on the bike can bring leg cramps and soreness. Most are mounted in front of the regular footpad, on the engine guard, or "crash bars," which I described above.

I couldn't afford the engine guard that I wanted, which had built-in highway pegs, so I had highway pegs mounted off the front end of my footpads, and they worked just fine.

I asked about styles and prices, and the cost to install them. One great idea the sales rep had was to consider buying comfort grip handles with matching throttle stops, since that was going to play into the basic comfort of the ride. He also made a case for the Air Hawk seat, gave a demonstration, and let me try it out. That changed my mind about it, so I decided to track down a used one on Craigslist instead of buying one at full price, about $110.

I felt a bit like Ralphie's little brother in the movie A Christmas Story when he's all dressed up for the snow and loudly complains, "I can't put my arms down!"

The sales rep also sent me home with a catalog to review, which was pretty dangerous. Later when I flipped through it, though, it didn't make me want to purchase more, but less. I found some really nice highway pegs that could attach to my existing footpads and still do the trick without the cost (or look) of crash bars. Still, I wanted to check a few more shops out before making a final decision, and on my way home, I realized I had chatted so long at the first shop that the second was no longer open.

I skipped on to the next thing on my shopping list, which was stopping in a few places to compare memory cards for a GoPro. As I said, my co-worker Joey had generously offered her GoPro for the trip, and I needed to make sure I had enough memory, and a way to mount it to my helmet or the bike for the ride. Target was the winner, with as 64GB card for a mere $29.99.

I hit a few other stores to check prices on rain suits, vests, gloves, and boots. My boots are great, but after six years, the bottoms were losing their grip, so best to get a new pair. I found some fingerless gloves I really liked for about $15.99 at Fleet Farm, and snatched them up. Joey said they were a good investment, and I had already discovered that you don't want to buy the cheapest ones you find.

I couldn't find any fitted ladies' vests that I liked, so I resigned myself to purchasing one online. I was warned to stay away from a particular brand of rain suit, so I had to look around quite a bit for something that would work. I have a great rain suit set, but when I tried to pull it on over my armored Tyvek jacket and leather chaps, it was a definite no-go. If I had already been wet, there would have been no way I could have pulled either the jacket or the pants on. I was going to have to either buy a ladies' large or extra-large, or a men's small. I felt a bit like Ralphie's little brother in the movie *A Christmas Story* when he's all dressed up for the snow and loudly complains, "I can't put my arms down!"

I had also spent part of my week reviewing videos on YouTube for best ways to pack for a long motorcycle trip, and tips for your first motorcycle trip. In doing so, I ran across a young woman who had crossed the country alone on a motorcycle, documenting it with a series of videos. I played them all in the background while I was organizing my notes for the ride. She's a great inspiration, and I hope to meet her someday. Her name is Amanda Zito, and her blog is called *As the Magpie Flies*. Check it out!

Another inspiring thing that occurred that week was that donations began coming in through my GoFundMe page. I had set it up as completely as I could, and posted links to it through Facebook, Twitter, and email, but not much happened after that. Then BAM! People started to notice it and began donating! I was so happy! I thought, "Jeez, no backing out now, I really have to go on this trip!"

Seriously, though, I couldn't have been more flattered by the pledges and comments coming in, and the amount of support. I wasn't sure any part of this was going to fly, apart from me just riding down and joining the group. So anything above and beyond that was gravy. At this point the trip was only two months and a week away, and I was starting to get excited . . . and nervous.

Packing Practice

First Weekend in April
62 Days to Kickstands Up!

My co-worker, Joey, had been on a few motorcycle trips, so she offered to loan me anything she had that I might need. How lucky was I? I immediately worked up a wish list and presented it to her. We had already discussed that I would borrow her GoPro camera, but there were a few other pricey items I still needed that might be borrowable, such as her rain suit.

I had tried to fit mine over my motorcycle jacket and chaps, but it was a tight fit, and if I had to put it on in the pouring rain, it would take even longer to climb into it. I laughed out loud when I pulled up the rain pants and they stopped at my behind. I'd never had a problem with this before in my life, and I found it hilarious. I paused for a moment, wrestled the pants up the rest of the way just to show them who's boss, and took a moment before figuring out how to get them off. The trick there turned out to be pulling both pairs of pants off in one move. And, fortunately, I didn't dislocate both shoulders trying to take off the rain jacket. Whew! What a workout, though.

Joey's rain paints were 3X and HUGE. I was sure they would work . . . as long as I stayed sitting down. I would need suspenders to hold them up if I needed to walk anywhere at all in them. I figured worn over chaps, they would manage to stay up on their own. Joey also had a bonus pair of boot covers that would be lovely to have in a monsoon. The rain pants had slits with Velcro tabs on the calves to easily slip over big boots, and the boot covers actually had stirrups and forefoot soles to boot, pun intended.

Joey also helped me out by ordering some of my requests online along with her yearly spring purchase so we could get free shipping. I needed cargo bungees, a face/neck mask for cold and wind, and ROK straps, none of which I could find locally. ROK straps allow you to run the strap around any part of the motorcycle and then back through a loop at the end of the strap, making virtually any part of the motorcycle a point of attachment. Then the two sections snap together in the center with a buckle.

I also had viewed a video that recommended compression wear to prevent muscle fatigue on long days, so I decided to get compression sleeves, but in a wild tattoo pattern of skulls and roses. I did this as a joke, since I am SO not a skulls-and-roses type of girl. I thought it would add a bit of fun to the ride. "Maybe I'll walk on the wild side for awhile just to see what it feels like!" I thought.

I asked a few more dumb questions on the ride's "Chatterbox" site on Facebook, created just for pre-ride yakking. How do other riders handle their cash and credit on the trip? Would it be wise to get cruise control installed? Full face or half helmet? When I asked the ladies how they managed money on the ride to get a consensus of how much they take in cash versus charging on credit, I got about a dozen different answers. When I asked which type of helmet would be better on the trip—full face or half—again a variety of answers. It started to become clear to me what "ride your own ride" meant. Whatever I was most comfortable in was the right thing to do, and it didn't matter how many others were doing it. It was nice to have the freedom to do so.

I even spent a good part of an hour chatting with Karen, the wonderful lady who organizes the trip year after year. She's a sweetheart and works hard getting sponsorships. One of the fun questions she asked on Facebook was what the ladies' road nicknames were. They were pretty colorful, and typically reflected something of the rider's personality. For example, "Jazz" got her name because she likes that type of music. The ladies also said if you didn't have one yet, you would before the ride was over.

I continued working on core exercises to help with my stamina, and they evolved as I kept at it. I kept a log of what I did and when I did it, so I could track my progress. When I finally pulled the bike out of the garage, I noticed a particular muscle in my bum wasn't very happy about pushing my 600-pound bike out onto the driveway, so I had to find a way to, um, build that up a bit.

During the week, I contacted a guy about 30 miles away on Craigslist who had a used Air Hawk seat for sale. An Air Hawk is a pad that straps onto your stock seat on the bike. It has baffles that inflate, and hold you just off the seat enough to get air flowing around your cheeks so you don't develop the "monkey butt" I referred to earlier. Another coworker had highly recommended it, and so had the shop in the other town. I hadn't planned on getting it, but it was clear my comfort was going to determine how much I enjoyed the ride, so I figured it was an excellent investment. My coworker had assured me that they really don't wear out, and would last a long time. Plus, this guy was selling it for about $30 less than a new one, and that was going to save money for something else I would need. I set up a meeting for Saturday afternoon.

Saturday morning I got up early, put my dog in the car, and drove to three counties looking for things I needed to modify my bike for the trip. I started out about 20 minutes from home at the dealership I bought my bike from. I spent an hour with three men, one of whom was the manager, and several catalogs trying to figure out exactly what I needed. In the end, they decided that the guy who had the answers wasn't there and he would call me back on Monday. Sheesh! Just forget it, guys. I returned to the car, and if my dog could've rolled her eyes at me, she probably would have.

About 10 minutes down the road, I realized I'd left my catalog behind, and I was upset about that, but I wasn't going back. We headed over to a town in another county, where there was a motorcycle shop that a friend had suggested I check out. The little shop was adorned with parts from old bikes, neatly displayed on the walls along with a few antique motorcycles on the floor. Unfortunately, it was a Harley-only shop, but I still had a nice chat with a guy I assume was the owner about old motorcycles and how cool they are. After a brief chat about the incompatibility of tools,

I pulled off the motorcycle cover, welcomed Xena out of her winter sleep, dropped the battery in, and she started right up. I pulled her out into the driveway and into the sun.

metric measurements and imported motorcycles, I told him thank you and went on my merry way. My merry way led me to a third county 30 miles north, where I was to purchase the Air Hawk seat.

Rick was a friendly guy. The Air Hawk was in great condition, and he said he had ridden less than 300 miles in it. We chatted a little bit about long-distance rides and I thanked him and then headed home. I took the long way home because it was a beautiful, 50-degree day. When we got back, I pulled off the motorcycle cover, welcomed Xena out of her winter sleep, dropped the battery in, and she started right up. I pulled her out into the driveway and into the sun. By then it was late afternoon, and a friend who happened to be walking by stopped and we had a long chat about the trip.

My friend found me trying to figure out where to place a fork bag that I've had for a few years and just never figured out exactly where I wanted it. Obviously not on the fork.

Fork bags are typically leather bags about the size of a small purse, with a zipper. They generally are made to fasten to the bike above the front tire, on the fork, the two parts of the frame that come down on either side of the front tire, attaching the front axle to the frame of the bike. I wanted a to be able to access my bag quickly, without getting off the bike, so I tried to find the best place to mount it to the bike where it would be accessible and yet not in the way.

It took me about three or four tries before I was happy with where it was. I eventually mounted it on the inside of the windshield so I could reach it easily at a stop. I cleaned out the saddlebags and took a long, hard look at my bike, trying to imagine how everything was going to work on the trip.

I woke up on Sunday, and in spite of the pain from a sinus headache, decided to take some medicine and do what was on the list for that day, which was to try and organize all my things and do a practice pack. I pulled everything from the staging area (and yes, I had a staging area) and put it all on my bed. I got out my checklists (yes, there were several and I eventually combined them). I also went through all my clothing to make sure it was polyester with wicking ability instead of cotton. For the record, it's exhausting to go through all the clothes in your closet and figure out what they're made of, but it does help you understand what is the best stuff to take on the trip.

About an hour into the pack, my head still hurt and I realized I had taken the wrong medicine, but the packing was going well. Everything looked like it was packed into freeze-dried packages. Was I going to the moon? I'm proud to say that only four items got cut from the packing pile. I took a "before" and "after" photo during this process, because the difference was so significant.

Everything fit nicely, and I was pleased. I didn't even need my smaller black duffel bag, which I thought I was definitely going to need. Two pair of shoes didn't make the cut, but they fit into my tactical backpack just fine.

My tactical backpack is one of my favorites. I have an affinity for organization, and anything that organizes efficiently delights me to no end. I didn't even know about tactical backpacks until my coworker Joey brought hers into work one day.

It was love at first sight.

It featured what seemed like dozens of little "cubbies" for storing all sorts of items. There were pockets of all sizes—some for pens, some for paper, some zippered, some mesh, some lined with soft material for sunglasses. There was a small, zippered pouch in front for easy access, and a sturdy handle at the top for carrying. The backside of the pack was lined with soft material to make it comfortable to wear even when filled with heavy gear. But the most wonderful thing about Joey's tactical backpack was that it was covered with canvas loops. Strips and strips of wonderfully efficient canvas loops. Loops that could attach at almost any point to a bungee cord, rubber strap, or carabiner clip. The possibilities were endless!

This is what made it the perfect thing for storage on a motorcycle. I bought two of them after Joey told me all about the magical aisle at Fleet Farm where the tactical bags lived.

There was also plenty of room for souvenir t-shirts and gifts that I planned to purchase on the trip. The rain gear fit neatly into my saddlebags, and I still had lots of room in my expandable tank bag. "You know, I think this may just work!" I teased myself.

Upon closer inspection, after attempting to zip up my duffel, I found the zipper pretty cranky, and it started to split open in the wrong places. That's when I realized how long I'd had that duffel bag, and that it was probably time to get a new one. I really didn't want my zipper splitting open in the middle of a deluge while I was doing 80 miles an hour down the road. I took measurements and found one on Fleet Farm's website

It must have been an entertaining sight, me opening all the little compartments and exclaiming at each new discovery. Most women don't do this in the sporting goods section of a store, or any store for that matter.

that was the right size, and also matched my tactical bag and all the loops for MOLLE modification. I was a little too excited about that, but I was even more excited when I found the bag at the store in my town.

The MOLLE system (pronounced similar to the name Molly) is an acronym for Modular Lightweight Load-carrying Equipment. Most MOLLE gear has webbing on each side, which provides multiple points for attaching gear on the rows and columns of the webbing with buckles or clips. Military personnel use this system to store and carry a myriad of necessities through rough terrain. There's websites featuring thousands of items to custom organize your pack for whatever you might be using it for, but I was afraid I would enjoy shopping on them a little too much, so I demonstrated some rare self-control and stuck with just the basic pack.

It must have been an entertaining sight, me opening all the little compartments of the duffel and exclaiming at each new discovery. Most women don't do this in the sporting goods section of a store, or any store for that matter. But this item was key to the entire operation, and I was pumped to have found it. The new duffel even had wheels, and an extending handle to pull it with. It was exactly what I needed. I gladly slapped the $70 down for the purchase.

The Preparations Continue

I guess it's part of being a writer, but I tend to geek out just about everything I do, especially so when I'm excited about it. I went to Mexico with a friend once and actually built a binder filled with itineraries, hotel information, and what the area we visited had to offer. I wanted to make sure we didn't miss a thing! I took the binder along but barely touched it while on the trip. I realized it was just my way of getting excited about my vacation, and didn't feel bad about ignoring it.

The same thing happened with this trip. The organizer of the trip had a good list, not just of items to bring but also how to prepare outside of that. She mentioned having a good helmet, good boots, a CamelBak for hydration, proper luggage and how to pack it for the weather, wicking shirts, having your bike in good working order, and being accustomed to any new modifications you might add before the trip. Riders who were veterans of past rides chimed in with other ideas they felt made the ride easier or more comfortable.

That was great, but not enough for me. I had to read dozens of articles online and watch endless videos of people packing for long rides to feel like I had really "beaten the bushes" for all the great ideas. When I saw the same tips suggested again and again, I knew they were used often and trusted by riders with a lot more experience that I had, and the best ones to follow.

I combined all the lists and then pared them down to what applied to me, and what I had room to pack.

Other tips that came in handy were exactly how to pack. To take only one or two of any clothing item, and wash along the way. Another suggestion was to take old clothes and simply discard them when they needed washing. Rolling clothes instead of folding and packing multi-use items or sharing a common item among roommates (like a container of the Anti Monkey Butt powder!), or simply leaving a questionable item behind, and buying it on the road if needed.

Another thing to be aware of was the weight of the pack, how it's distributed, and how it affects the bike's tires and suspension, and thus the ride. Motorcycles and luggage racks have weight limits, and it's imperative not to overburden the bike. Keeping the load as low as possible is important and sometimes challenging, so practicing the packing was serious business.

I started taking regular long rides with the bike packed for the trip so I could get used to how the load affected acceleration, cornering, and stopping. It also helped my body and my mind get used to long hours in the saddle, and various weather conditions. Unless it was dangerous to ride, I did my best to get my miles in, knowing it would make me a better rider on the trip.

The Other Side of the Ride

In the months and weeks leading up to the ride, Karen Collins, the ride's organizer, would post countdowns as the ride got closer. She'd continue to announce the numbers for the ride as registrations came in, and mention last-minute details as well as new sponsors for the ride. Sponsors provide lunch or dinner for the riders and many times a much-needed snack break in mid-morning or mid-afternoon. The dealerships promote the charity we're riding for in the local area and invite local riders to stop out and meet the ladies of the Women's Freedom Ride.

At several stops, we were to be welcomed and escorted in by a group of local riders or police officers. Talk about the red carpet treatment!

When a new rider signed up for the ride, Karen would post her name on the Facebook page for the ride and ask us to welcome her, and we would, enthusiastically. At one point, there were 51 women signed up for the ride. "Welcome, Wind Sister!" was a typical response. "Looking forward to meeting you and riding together!" was another. I would usually take the time to stop by their Facebook page to attach a face to the new name. There would almost always be a shot of the lady and her ride, and there were a lot of big, beautiful bikes on this ride.

During the weeks leading up to the ride, Karen asked us to send in a photo of ourselves with our bikes so she could create a poster to help promote the ride and also as a souvenir of our participation. The poster featured a calendar that showed which states we would be in for the duration of the ride.

Meanwhile, the Facebook thread was buzzing with riders asking questions about the nuts and bolts of the ride, and about gear that the ladies liked and wanted to share with others. Ladies were exchanging gear at no cost, things they no longer used. Gloves, boots, helmets, jackets . . . plus there was lots of great advice to share as well. Every once in a while, a countdown would pop up of how many days were left before the ride began, or until "Kickstands Up," which is typical motorcycle lingo for the exact time the group is heading out.

Other good suggestions were shared, such as making a journal of the ride, or sending postcards from each city we stop in. Purple bandanas symbolized the cause we were riding for, so the ladies stocked up on those and all things purple, reporting where the best deal on them could be found.

Final Preparations

April 13
46 Days to Kickstands Up!

I took the time to combine all 4.5 packing lists into one, organized by where items were packed on bike: left saddlebag, right saddlebag, duffel, backpack, tank bag, fork bag, me. You might not think this is a big deal, but when you have to find something very quickly while parked on the side of the road with semis flying past, or with 30-plus women on motorcycles waiting on you to leave, it definitely is. You don't want to be reaching into your left saddlebag on a busy highway, you want to be on the right side of your bike, for obvious reasons.

The dealership's annual checkup on the bike was complete, but I made the mistake of scheduling it on Good Friday afternoon, and the trip back home could have been fatal. Too many people trying to beat it home for the holiday weekend, and very distracted. Good news: my list of needs was getting shorter, thanks to everyone helping out.

At the time of the ride, I was writing for a newspaper, and had mentioned in my weekly column some of the items I was looking for and having trouble finding. Once in a while, I would find things waiting for me on my front porch, like the day I came home and found a container of the Anti-Monkey Butt powder one of the ladies on Facebook had mentioned. There was no note, but a few days later a friend of mine confessed that she found it at a local store and had to get it for me.

Now that the bike checkup was complete, I took the bike in for modifications to a local shop in my town. Riders who had been on long rides told me that as long as my hands, seat, and feet were comfortable, I should have no trouble covering all those miles on the ride. I had the seat comfort covered with the Air Hawk seat, so I purchased hand grips that were softer and shaped for an easier grip. I added throttle stops and also did a little research on highway pegs, found some that I liked, and had those attached to my footpads.

I spent a lot of money that week, that's for sure. Modifications done, I repacked everything into the awesome new duffel bag and made my first attempt at packing the bike for the trip. Everything went well, and the ride was amazingly comfortable. Why hadn't I done this years ago? My first real practice ride was a great success! Paying off the credit card was going to be a little bit tougher.

First Week of May
35 Days to Kickstands Up!

Activity on the ride's Facebook page was more and more frequent as excitement began to grow. Occasionally someone would post a screenshot of the countdown of days to the start of the ride. The poster for the ride had been printed, and everyone was excited to see it.

"Can't wait to see everyone. I'm ready."
— Martha V. Phelan

"Remember to bring your motorcycle license, registration and insurance card!"
— Penny Hurt

"I ran my printer out of ink printing hard copies of my mapquesting . . . "
— Mary Dickinson

"Just wondering, is anyone bringing or wearing their leather vest?"
— Anja O'Brien

"Where is everyone joining us, and how far are you going?"
— Jean Everly

"Ladies! Take a pic of your odometer for scrapbooking!!"
— Sabrina Tippins

"Somebody talk me down . . . anticipation is about to whoop my butt!!"
— Mary Dickinson

A tattoo had been designed for the ride, and there's a different design each year. It's not a requirement to get one, but I was surprised how many women volunteered to do so. The design was the symbol for infinity, with the word "sisters" in the center, and a feather along the lower right loop of the symbol. Of course, the color purple runs through the entire design, as it's the color that represents the Women's Freedom Ride.

But now there was a slight problem: I was in Wisconsin,

and Mother Nature was not letting spring start. The weather continued to be cold and wet, which did not inspire me to head out and ride for several hours. Nonetheless, progress for the ride continued, albeit indoors.

I spent the time learning how a GoPro camera works (borrowed from my generous buddy, Joey) and purchased SD cards to store all the footage on.

On this ride, I would not only be expected to be ready to go at this crazy time of day, I'd be expected to ride regardless of my mood or the weather conditions, for hours without stopping, at high speeds, in high traffic.

I also worked a lot with Google maps to plan two to four-hour rides around central Wisconsin. It was a chore, since Google doesn't like circular routes, but I managed.

One Sunday's practice ride was phenomenal! I tried a new packing/mounting system that worked beautifully. Previously, the backpacks I used beneath the duffel put weight on the soft saddlebags and dented them, and I didn't like that. So I had to devise a system to hold them across the back seat like a saddle. Getting a second tactical bag was the answer. Both had clips down the sides, so I basically clipped them to each other and used a carabiner to attach them to the seat strap for extra insurance. They balanced out the duffel nicely, and I was very pleased. I also used the bungee nets to store my extra jacket.

It was a good thing I did, because only after a half hour or so, I needed to stop and switch out for my warmest gloves and my heavy jacket. Yes, this was springtime in Wisconsin, all right. The wind was something else, and battered me around, but the sun was out and it was a beautiful ride. The rolling countryside beneath the deep blue sky, with awesome views greeting me around each hillside and bend in the road made it a happy and satisfying run.

I didn't stop to take any on-the-road photos, as I was trying to mimic a two-hour ride without stopping. Still, I had to stop to change jackets, and eventually gas up. With each practice ride, I could feel my confidence building.

Third Week of May
18 Days to Kickstands Up!

The ladies on the Women's Freedom Ride Chatterbox page were anxiously counting the days to "kickstands up," and I had to admit, I was getting a tad anxious myself. What I didn't expect, though, was a foreign feeling that took me a bit of time to figure out. It showed up as a feeling of reluctance to ride, which puzzled me, since I love to ride, and I knew it was important to practice riding in full gear with a full load on the bike. "Why am I putting off practice riding?" I thought.

What it turned out to be was a combination of things. Generally, I'm used to riding in perfect conditions, when I feel like going for a ride. The sun is out, I feel good, well rested, happy. On this ride, I would have to be dressed, fed, packed, and on the bike by 7 a.m. most mornings. Did I mention I'm not a morning person?

On this ride, I would not only be expected to be ready to go at this crazy time of day, I'd be expected to ride regardless of my mood or the weather conditions, for hours without stopping, at high speeds, in high traffic. That's what makes the practice part so difficult, trying to duplicate those conditions.

Heading out for two hours and driving to Green Bay or

La Crosse on my own was out of the question. If something went wrong, I would be far from home and have to burden someone with coming to my rescue. I also wasn't happy about riding alone on highways, since single riders can be hard for drivers to see at high speeds. In large groups, it's no problem. Riding together is similar to behaving like a school of fish, and for similar reasons. Together we are more likely to be seen and respected, and if something goes wrong, there's a pool of knowledge and resources to come to your aid.

So I got creative with my trip planning and traveled in "wedges" instead. I would head out on secondary roads for a half hour to an hour in one direction (like northwest), then change and head directly east for another half hour or 45 minutes, and then head home. That way I was never very far from base camp and if things went sour, like the rain that fell on an already ridiculously cold Sunday, I could cut the ride short. "Wedging" also kept me riding in areas I was already familiar with, which helped keep my confidence up. It was also helpful when it came to knowing where I could gas up en route if necessary.

The benefits of spending summers camping with my parents was paying off in a big way. My Dad loved to plan trips, and because my mother couldn't read a map to save her life, I was Dad's navigator. He would hand me the extremely thick Woodall's camp guide, and it was my job to choose a campground and navigate him to it. That's a lot of trust to give to a fifth grader. I always chose the one with a pool.

I'm not typically superstitious, but I like to make note of good omens when they happen. As soon as I had finished the first practice pack of the bike, I noticed a little white butterfly flitting all around my bike for a few minutes. I thought that was a very good sign. I notice good omens while out riding as well, typically birds soaring overhead. I don't know why, but I seem to see them in sets of three. On one Sunday ride, a hawk, an eagle, and, of all things, a turkey flew over my head. Thankfully, they didn't leave any "calling cards" on me, or the bike.

There was a fearlessness I felt. A confidence. A sense that no matter what happened, everything would be just fine. Even if something went wrong, it would still be just fine.

The GoFundMe I created continued to grow, funded by some surprising donors, including my hometown's mayor! I thanked each and every one, since I really had zero expectations when I set up the page. In case you are curious, GoFundMe is not without fees and charges. Such an amazing platform does not come without strings attached. Each online donation is charged 7.9 percent, plus 30 cents. Five percent of that is for the GoFundMe platform, and 2.9 percent is for the company that transfers the money to an account that I could access. I forget what the 30 cents was for, but it doesn't matter, because without this platform, I would have had zero time to raise any funds at all.

However, sometimes the funds found me! During a stop at the chiropractor to make sure my back was in the best shape it could be for the ride, I mentioned the ride to the ladies at the desk as I was paying my bill. They were very excited and asked a lot of questions.

"Oh, how exciting! Where are you going?"
"What are you raising money for?"
"How long will you be gone?"

"How far does the ride go?"

"When does the ride start?"

All were typical questions of anyone who heard I was participating in the ride. What blew me away was the $60 they donated to the cause, which really touched me. This was just one of the many times a friend or acquaintance would randomly hand me money for the fundraiser after a chat about the ride. I think a lot of people were just plain stunned that someone like me would attempt such a feat, and I was always stunned by their generosity and faith in what I could do. It spurred me on with even more motivation as the last weeks before the ride came and went.

Time management has never been my strong suit. Another week went by, and suddenly it was a week before the ride! On Monday, I started to realize how short time was getting. I went in for my usual summer pedicure, and chose purple, since that's the color for the ride. On Tuesday, I started waking up at 6 a.m. without the alarm. I used my extra time in the morning before work to set up an entire room to stage the final packing process. On Wednesday, I waxed all the zippers on my duffel and backpacks so they moved easily, and rinsed out my brand new CamelBak and hung it up it to dry. CamelBaks were one of the items suggested on the list, to keep properly hydrated on the ride.

On Thursday, I was a bit reflective. The beginning of my ride was a little more than a week away and some interesting things were happening. I was starting to receive a lot of donations by hand . . . gifts and surprises, lots of support. Also interesting, I felt very calm and happy and peaceful. I could sense that this experience was going to change me in a big way, forever. It was a good feeling, and I was ready for it. And yes, I was a little bit afraid. But underlying everything was an amazing feeling that I'd reached some kind of new level. Some sort of rite of passage? There was a fearlessness I felt. A confidence. A sense that no matter what happened, everything would be just fine. Even if something went wrong, it would still be just fine.

And one strange thing. I keep having this nostalgic feeling, like I used to get when about to leave on vacation with my parents as a child. It was just so strange. A feeling I hadn't felt in a very long time, yet so familiar. I felt young, light-hearted, curious and excited. Not sure why that was popping up, but it happened a handful of times, so it wasn't a fluke.

Maybe Mom and Dad were trying to tell me something.

I'd lost my mom when I was a junior in high school. I came home from an afternoon of shopping with a friend to find my father with his arm around her, trying to hold her up as they both sat on the couch. He couldn't get her to respond and asked me to try. She had tried to get up from the couch, he said, and suddenly fell back, and now he couldn't get her to respond to him.

I called her name, and she seemed to hear me, but couldn't reply, and she kept rubbing the outside of her right leg with her left hand. What we didn't realize was that she was trying to tell us that she couldn't feel it anymore.

After taking her to the hospital, we were told she'd had a stroke, a blood clot to the brain. She stayed in a coma for four days, my father never leaving her side, refusing to go home to sleep. When she woke up, she had temporarily lost her ability to speak, but would hum responses back, using inflection to get her meaning across.

They told us it would take her a while to heal, and that she would regain the ability to speak, and the use of the right side of her body eventually.

But that never happened.

Two weeks later she had another stroke, but this time it was a stroke on the other side of her brain. It effectively knocked out the use of the rest of her body. They told us she would be in a vegetable-like state from now on. Hearing that as a teenager was more than I was willing to deal with. My father immediately began making plans to get a hospital bed at home for her comfort, and a vehicle equipped to take her on outings, and he made general plans to incorporate my mother's new disabilities into our lives.

But that never happened, either.

Two weeks later my mother had a third stroke—a hemorrhage, which meant bleeding in the brain. The doctors told us there was nothing they could do for her, and that it was only a matter of hours that she would live.

My mom always knew somehow that she wouldn't live to a ripe old age, and had always told us if she was in that sort of situation, to "pull the plug" on her. Of course we told her to stop talking nonsense and would change the subject. But here we were in that exact situation, and no one had the courage to follow her wishes. It was really my father's call anyway, and it was clear he wasn't about to do anything that would take her from him, no matter what.

My mother was a very strong-willed lady, and, in my opinion, she pulled her own plug. I have no doubt that somewhere deep inside, she was still there and frustrated as hell. There was no other way than to take care of it herself.

A month after my mother had taken ill, she was gone.

My father would live on until he was 84, although the last decade of his life he suffered from several small strokes, and also dementia.

My father never did approve of me riding a motorcycle. When I bought my Yamaha 950 in 2010, my stepmother Rosemary was excited and wanted to tell my dad. I asked her not to, because I didn't want him to worry. But she couldn't resist, and one day, when the family was out for a meal at a restaurant, she dropped the news over dessert.

My father just put his head down and kept eating his soup, saying nothing. I looked at her and said, "I told you so."

I hoped the dementia would be a blessing at that point and that he would forget what she had told him.

In the days leading up to the ride, I thought that perhaps the seemingly random nostalgic feeling I was experiencing was their way of nodding their approval. It spurred me on and inspired me to keep up with the practice rides and further fueled my preparation activities in those final weeks before it was time to go.

The following weekend was spent finalizing all the details and making sure everything had been purchased, acquired, and packed where it needed to be for the ride—we are talking Ninja Level Packing here. My friend Ginny, who has a wild sense of humor, dropped in with an unexpected gift: a "Bike Bubbler," a plastic contraption made for a bicycle that automatically creates "a magic trail of bubbles as you ride" down the road. We had a good laugh about that, and part of me really wished there was a place to attach it to Xena.

Less than a week to "kickstands up" and ETD (Estimated Time of Departure) was set for Saturday morning, June 3 . . . if the weather cooperated. With less than a week to go, it looked like 70 and sunny for that Saturday morning—absolutely perfect riding weather.

The Grand Adventure Begins!

I snuck out of town a day early, due to storms that were forecast for Saturday. I spent the morning finalizing the packing and paying bills that were due while I would be gone. I was sad to leave my pup, and nervous . . . very nervous about the trip. I was on the highway for about half hour before I finally started to relax and enjoy myself and the beautiful blue sky.

The sky is important when you're on a motorcycle, and you pay attention to it. Things can change quickly, so you need to stay aware. Scents in the air are another thing that stand out on a ride, and as I rolled along I noted the welcome smells of lilacs, campfires and outdoor grilling, and the not-so-welcome smells of manure, roadkill and stogies.

The only hazard I ran into was a turkey that crossed the road at a very inopportune moment, but neither biker nor bird was affected.

I checked in to a hotel just north of Janesville, WI. I was meeting my big sister Linda there. Linda lives near Racine and volunteered to accompany me to Paducah in her car. I was a bit reluctant to accept her help, wanting to do the ride entirely on my own. But when she jokingly told me, "You're the youngest—you can't die first," I laughed and agreed to it.

In Paducah I would rendezvous with the group, which would be headed to Paducah from Charleston on Sunday evening.

Linda and I had a great dinner at Quaker Steak & Lube, and later in the room, I took the opportunity to repack a bit more efficiently, leaving some things with Linda.

Saturday morning the sky to the north was dark—the rain I was hoping to miss. As I packed the bike, Linda offered to put some of it in her trunk, but I refused. I had planned for this, and was going to handle it as if I were on my own.

We got on the road early and got out from under the dark clouds quickly, gassing up once the skies cleared. The idea was that Linda would navigate with her GPS, and I would follow and only need to worry about traffic. That way we could take the interstate and make good time.

The plan worked well. Only one toll around Rockford, Illinois, that was awkward on the bike. When I needed to get Linda's attention, which wasn't often, I could overtake her, flash my high beams, or beep my horn. When we stopped to eat, I wanted to be able to see the bike from our table.

Every once in a while, when people come across a motorcycle in a parking lot, they find it amusing to put a young child on the bike and take photos without asking permission first. This can sometimes lead to injuries, because the exhaust pipes are hot and can burn little legs. Well-meaning admirers can cause damage if they aren't careful and end up knocking the bike over in their enthusiasm. It's always best to not touch a motorcycle without asking permission. It's actually a very personal possession, and should be regarded as much.

From the looks of others

Didn't they know I was a grandmother from Wisconsin who worked for a newspaper? Not dressed like this, they didn't.

around us in the restaurant, I was starting to become aware of how differently I was being perceived in my "biker" attire.

Although there are motorcyclists out there who wear leather to be cool and intimidating, leather is an important item of protection on the road. "Dress for the slide and not for the ride" is what they say, and it's important to pay heed. Leather not only protects you if you drop the bike, it also keeps you warm. There's also an acronym, ATGATT, which stands for All The Gear, All The Time. That's also important, since you never know when an accident will happen, regardless of how aware and experienced you are.

I'm one of those riders who wear all the gear, all the time. This is difficult when it's 90 degrees or warmer, as there's no "wind chill" effect at that speed or higher. Add the heat coming up off the engine, and riding on a hot summer day can be like riding in an oven. Still, you need to have leathers for protection.

Sitting in the restaurant perusing the menu with my big sis, I was dressed in full-length leather chaps and heavy riding boots, with a leather vest over my shirt, all black. On my head I wore a purple bandanna, which represented the color of the Women's Freedom Ride, also covered up my horrendous "helmet hair." I had a neckerchief around my neck, with a little angel pin my friend Jeanette had given me for protection. I had left my black Tyvek jacket and fingerless leather gloves on the bike, along with my helmet.

As I looked around the room to take in the ambiance, I noticed more than a few people giving me a sidelong glance, afraid to make long eye contact. It made me giggle. Didn't they know I was a grandmother from Wisconsin who worked for a newspaper? Not dressed like this, they didn't.

I smiled a warm, friendly smile back at each one of them, and they quickly looked away. Hey, I tried.

We arrived in Bloomington Saturday early afternoon, and while my sister suggested about a dozen things to do there, I just wanted to nap. I was sorry to disappoint her, but riding in the wind all day had been exhausting, physically and mentally, and I just wanted to sleep. Later we enjoyed a lovely dinner together at DESTIHL Restaurant and Brew Works, and back at the room, I continued to purge and repack.

We set out the next day and lunched in Effingham, Illinois, at the Gabby Goat, a great place to eat if you're ever in the area. I loved the name of the town because every time you said it, it sounded like you were cussing. Again, I noticed the looks from others in the restaurant and parking lot and was amused. I certainly didn't think I looked very threatening.

After lunch we headed south, aware that we were going to run into some weather. As we neared Paducah, the skies grew increasingly black and agitated, and it became clear I wasn't going to beat it. At one point the temperature dropped suddenly, the wind came up and I said to myself, "Here we go!" and the rains came.

The summer air was filled with the smell of cool rain hitting hot pavement. I was fine with it until the lightning started. I started beeping my horn and gesturing to Linda to pull off, which she did. She pulled onto the shoulder about midway up the ramp, and I jumped off the bike with thunder crashing all around and slid into her front seat, laughing. Linda immediately got on her phone and started checking the weather radar.

"It looks like it's going to pass. We're right on the edge of it," she said.

"Great," I said, "let's give it a few minutes and let this downpour pass through and then we'll head out."

I told her how intimidating it felt to be riding at full speed toward the black clouds in front of us on the highway.

"I've never done that before, since I only ride when the weather is good," I said.

Riding into the storm was both scary and exhilarating at the same time. I could actually feel the temperature drop as we got closer to the front, and I could smell the rain about thirty seconds before it came down.

Not having a lot of experience riding in the rain, much less a heavy one, I decided it was best to sit it out, since we had some time to spare. We waited about ten minutes and when the rain let up, we headed down the road again.

I was excited to be so close, only about 30 minutes from Paducah, when another cloudburst hit. We pulled off again, and this time it came down even harder, and other cars also pulled off the road. We waited for what seemed like a long time, but the storm cell seemed stalled over us, and radar showed that just south of us the skies were clear.

"What do you want to do?" Linda asked. "It's your call."

"I really don't want to miss the girls pulling in to the hotel when they arrive." I said. "I think we should just go for it." I said it, but I still didn't really feel I was ready to go.

"Whatever you think," Linda said, "It's up to you."

Eventually my anxiety over missing the ride's arrival overcame my fear of the lightning and thunder that had subsided, but still flashed and crashed all around us. Knowing the other riders were in the same storm system as they approached from the south gave me courage. If they were doing it, so could I.

"Let's just go for it." I told her. "Okay!" she said.

About 10 minutes down the road, the rain stopped, and we arrived shortly in Paducah. The group hadn't arrived yet, as they had been riding through storms all day as well and had been delayed.

As I took my luggage off the wet bike, Linda tried to help.

"Don't be my valet!" I snapped at her. She looked at me with a puzzled expression.

"I have no idea what these women are like, and I don't want to come across as weak. First impressions and all, you know." I explained.

"All right, whatever you want," Linda replied.

"Here, you can carry this," I said, as I handed her a small green tote bag. "The rest is mine."

I put on my best stoic biker face and strolled into the lobby, trying to be as nonchalant as possible. Looking around the room, I could see I was embarrassingly overpacked, and did my best to hide the amount of luggage I had brought in. There were about a half dozen women also waiting for the ride to arrive, and they all had quite different looks. I wasn't sure what kind of conversation to initiate.

It wasn't long though, before the girls noticed my overabundance of stuff, and made some teasing comments about it. The thing was, we really didn't know each other well enough for that just yet, so I was still trying to be as polite as I could with my responses.

"I just brought what was on the list," I said defensively.

"There was a LIST?" One of them replied snarkily.

Not knowing what to say, I simply nodded.

"Well, some of us *wash* our clothes," said another.

Hoo, boy. If the next two weeks were going to go as well as this, I was in for a *very* long trip.

You can imagine the relief I felt when the sound of motorcycle engines began to fill the air outside.

We stepped outside under the canopy of the hotel to watch more than a dozen drenched riders roll in. The rain hadn't dampened their spirits, though. They were a loud, rowdy bunch and clearly happy to be at their destination. I marveled at the variety of women and the bikes they rode.

There were riders from all walks of life, in a variety of ages. A little concerned I might be one of the oldest on the ride, I eventually learned that two of the women on our ride were in their 70s! Big touring bikes with large fairings, small bikes without even a windshield, sport bikes, and a handful of trikes, in all manner of customization. But they all had one thing in common: a tightly-stuffed pack of basic belongings strapped to their machine, and most had some form of purple decorating their ride, like a purple bandanna hanging from a handlebars, backrest or tail light.

Some of the group went to check in, and some unloaded their bikes amid happy hoots and hollers and hugs. I stood amidst the seeming chaos and started to feel overwhelmed. What had I gotten myself into?

I turned to my sister and quietly joked, "I'm a little bit out of my league, don't you think?"

Linda paused for a moment, then walked around to face me and said, "You know what? I'm proud of you!"

"You are?!" I responded.

She gave me a big hug, and before our tears could flow, she walked to her car without looking back, and drove off. Stunned, and filled with a dozen emotions at that moment, I thought, "Okay, let's do this!"

0 to 85 mph in 24 Hours, or . . .
It's Not a Learning Curve, It's a Cliff!

Standing under the canopy of the hotel, I wasn't quite sure what the next step was. I stood there with a friendly look on my face, figuring that after the welcomes calmed down, someone might introduce herself. That person was Linda.

"Hi!" she said, "I'm Linda, but my nickname is "Jazz," because I like jazz music. I'm from Tennessee."

I would come to know many of the ladies on the ride by their "road names," and some only exclusively that way. The next person to introduce herself was Mary, who joyfully spouted, "I'll hug you if you want me to!" Which was probably the last thing I ever thought I'd hear from a biker girl.

I knew the names of my roommates, but their images only from Facebook. Figuring out who they were in a sea of women trying to check in was a challenge. I did manage to identify a few, since I am really good with faces.

I spotted Annette, a stylish, tall blonde in the line. I assumed that roommates most likely hung together, so I scanned the line around Annette for the other two. I wanted to be sure before I approached anyone. I couldn't find Karen anywhere in the group at all, then I spotted Diane, who was busy joking and chatting with the ladies nearby her in line. That made her look approachable, so I walked up and simply said, "Hi . . . are you Diane?"

When she nodded, I introduced myself. "Hi, I'm your new roommate from Wisconsin. I'm Paula!" Her face lit up with recognition, since we had chatted a bit about the room details on Facebook chat in the past months.

She welcomed me to the ride and then directed me to Karen, the woman who had made all our reservations. She was a smaller, dark-haired woman at the front of the line trying to check in and get room keys for everyone, and she seemed stressed. The whole scene was chaotic, so I just sat down in the lobby with my bags until things began to calm down and thin out.

I eventually got a room key and hauled everything up to the room, trying to blend in as casually as possible with my new friends. In the room, I chatted with my roommates Annette and Diane for a while and realized how odd it was that I was spending the night with virtual strangers. Eventually Annette left to socialize with the group, and Diane and I chatted a bit. When she noticed my compression socks, she told me that if I needed any meds for muscle cramps and the like during the ride, that she was happy to share.

I did my best to blend in but didn't feel like I was doing a very good job of it. I did a lot of observing and kept my mouth shut, always a good plan.

When Karen finally got up to the room, she was flustered, and told a story of the accident she'd had that day on the road. Her trike kit had failed, and she had lost a wheel, steering the bike as best she could to the shoulder. A trike kit is equipment that converts a regular, two-wheeled motorcycle into a tricycle with three wheels, one in the front, and two in the back. It's popular with riders who are concerned about balance, and dropping the bike, since you can't "drop" a trike.

No one had been hurt, but it did shake everyone up, especially Karen. Not only that, but a second accident had occurred that day on the ride. A van had lost a tire, and it had rolled into the group as it travelled down the road. Thankfully, no one was injured in the incident.

Karen was last to arrive to the room because she had been down at the trailer working on the bike with Jeffrey, our mechanic.

A Purple Heart recipient and the only man on the ride, Jeffrey drove the chase vehicle filled with tools, water, and promotional materials. When Karen finally caught her breath, she noticed me, smiled and gave me a big, welcoming hug. I was starting to feel like part of the group… just a little.

We decided bed assignments, and I put my things away in my corner of the room. Karen and I would be bed buddies for the rest of the trip. We didn't have a lot of time to get to know each other that night, due to the fact that she was working on her bike with Jeff until the late hours of the night. I took a shower and relaxed for an hour or so before bedtime, wondering what the morning ride would bring.

Monday, June 5
Paducah, Kentucky, to Blue Springs, Missouri

I awoke at 5:30 a.m. to the sound of thunder and the rustling of plastic bags. I got dressed, loaded the bike, then relaxed over breakfast. I did my best to blend in but didn't feel like I was doing a very good job of it. I did a lot of observing and kept my mouth shut, always a good plan.

The rain was expected to continue. As I mentioned earlier, I had borrowed my coworker Joey's gear, which was way too big for me, but found a way to wear it so that the pants didn't fall down. The rain gear also covered my boots, which felt a little bit like wearing flippers. Outside under the hotel canopy, we met a half hour before "kickstands up," when all riders are expected to be done with bathroom needs and bike packing, dressed properly, with helmet on and astride a running motorcycle.

This was the morning briefing, where we would get information about what day it was, the route we were taking, the weather, and any hazards, traffic, or other problems we would need to be aware of.

Six new riders had joined the group, so we reviewed the hand signals we would be using on the road. Left turn, right turn, slow down, speed up, police ahead, single file, and regular formation. Regular formation was also reviewed: to stagger our positions on the left and right side of the lane, and not to ride side by side. This gave us room to maneuver easily within the lane to avoid debris on the road, or, God forbid, an animal running across the road or a loose tire from a semi truck. We were also instructed to leave the proper amount of space between ourselves – one second of time between ourselves and the rider on the other side of the lane, and two seconds of time between ourselves and the rider in front of us. The briefing ended with a prayer circle, all holding hands, asking for a safe ride and also that military folk be brought back to their families safely.

"May the sun rise in front of us, the rain fall behind us, and the wind follow us. May the angels guard our travels, for they know what is ahead of us. Keep us safe through rolling hills and

swirling turns. Let the eagle guide us to the mountaintops and let the moon's light guide us through the night. Lord, thank you for letting us be bikers. We ask that you keep our loved ones safe while we are away. We also ask that you keep all military at home and overseas wrapped in your loving arms."

    It seemed like forever before we were ready to go. While waiting, I chatted briefly with a gentleman motorcyclist from Ohio who was on his way to California. He asked about the ride and I told him about our cause, and before I knew it, he was handing me a $5 donation. This would come to be a very common occurrence during the ride, as 30-some women riders preparing for the day's ride is quite a spectacle, and many folks were interested and supportive.

    I didn't realize we needed to line up properly, but my roommate, Annette, who rode a trike, saw me in the wrong spot and gave me a heads up. She told me that trikes ride in the back and I would need to line up with the two-wheeled bikes. I nodded to her to show I understood and looped around the parking lot to the proper position, at the back of the line of the two-wheeled motorcycles. Listening to all the engines fire up was exhilarating and also made me nervous. What had I gotten myself into? Was I going to be able to pull this off? Too late to worry about that now.

You never really think about the length of a stoplight sitting in your car on a hot day, but holding up a 600-pound motorcycle on hot asphalt on a ninety-degree day, it becomes an issue.

    The ride captains put their thumbs in the air and looked for a return of the same sign. The ladies put their thumbs in the air, and when it was unanimous, it was time to ride.

Riding a Yamaha in a sea of Harleys has always been amusing for me. I can't hear my own engine, so I have to pay close attention when shifting. I kicked it into first, let the clutch out to the friction point, and waited for the line to move. As we pulled out of the hotel parking lot, the chase vehicle held traffic while we entered the street, and a few people took videos of our departure. Using our hand signals, we entered the highway at a slower speed, and once all the riders were together, we took off down the road.

Most of that first day is a blur to me, since I was so nervous I could barely function. Trying to keep up to speed so there were no gaps, trying to maintain the proper distance, and watching for hand signals and road hazards took up so much of my brain that many times I was barely aware of the traffic around us. Or worse, it would startle me as it passed by, adding to the stress I was already feeling.

Our first stop was at Black Diamond Harley-Davidson in Marion, Illinois. They were to have "refreshments" for us, but seemed to have forgotten we were coming. After a short wait, we were treated to Krispy Kreme donuts and hot coffee. Of course, many of the girls did some shopping while we waited, or perhaps that was part of the forgotten donut strategy.

A Yamaha girl hasn't much to do at a HD dealership, so I hung outside and admired the other girls' bikes. I watched carefully what the other riders did during the stop. As I was strolling past the bikes parked at the front of the dealership, I was shocked to see Jean, one of the ride captains, had pulled off her gas tank! I was too intimidated to ask what was wrong, and to be honest,

I didn't even realize they came off, so I tried to be cool and not look as surprised as I felt. I was feeling pretty inadequate at that point, since I can't even change my bike's oil, but I later learned that Jean works on C17s for the air force, so it made sense she would be able to take apart a motorcycle with confidence.

We were split into two groups to better navigate the traffic of St. Louis, and put 10 minutes between the groups' departures. I did see the famous arch from a distance away but was too focused on traffic to be impressed. I was impressed, however, by the beautiful design of the Stan Musial Veterans Memorial Bridge we crossed on the way to St. Charles Harley-Davidson in St. Charles, where we ate a wonderful lunch provided by the dealership. It was a basic lunch of sub sandwiches, chips, soda, and soft cookies for dessert, but after my stressful morning in the hot temperatures, it was like manna from heaven.

After enjoying lunch, I made conversation with the other ladies at the table and relaxed in the lovely air-conditioned shop. I commented on how great it felt. Karen, the ride's organizer who's lovingly referred to as "Momma Bear," flatly told me with a smirk on her face, "Don't get used to it."

The day had grown quite warm for this Wisconsin girl. You never really think about the length of a stoplight sitting in your car on a hot day, but holding up a 600-pound motorcycle on hot asphalt on a ninety-degree day, it becomes an issue. I had to literally peel off my jacket when I got to the dealership. I didn't want to ride without protection, so I kept the front of my jacket unzipped and used my new CamelBak regularly. I found that drinking water throughout the day also kept me focused when my attention began to waver, as did singing to myself inside my helmet.

And yes, even in the middle of the day—at 75 mph on the open road amid a bevy of roaring motorcycles—your body can start to relax a little too much, and you look for ways to stay alert. I found myself singing silly songs I recalled from Girl Scouts and summer playground bus trips. I sang all sorts of Tom Pease songs that I remembered from when my children were young. I sang folk songs and patriotic songs. It's quite fun to sing "God Bless America" as loud as you like when no one can hear it over the roar of your engine. The trade-off? You're going to use up a lot more water when you have your mouth open that much at highway speeds.

Trip planning in February

Pre-ride bike pack and test ride

Testing the GoPro

A gift of Monkey Butt Powder from a fan

First practice pack

Modifications for comfort: highway pegs

Modifications for comfort: Soft, friendly hand grips and throttle stop

MOLLE backpack and new duffel bag

Dot-to-Dot map I created for my grandchildren to follow

My trusty steed and I, leaving Janesville, Wisconsin

The morning we left Paducah, Kentucky, where I joined the group; still raining

A typical gas stop on the ride

Jeffrey, a Purple Heart Recipient, the only man allowed on the ride with the chase vehicle and trailer; our mechanic, backup, and water boy.

Sabrina, one of the ride captains, explains how to best fill in gaps in the line

Negotiating toll booths is a bit awkward with a group of riders

Bikes lined up outside the veterans home in Topeka, Kansas

Ladies enjoying lunch at the Evel Knievel Museum in Topeka, Kansas

Jazz poses for the camera with her copilot in Hays, Kansas

Gathering for the morning meeting in Hays, Kansas

Important warning on the back of the trailer on our chase vehicle

Another typical gas stop on the ride; that's me and Xena on the left

The ladies pose with a future rider at our hotel in Fort Collins (Photo courtesy of Karen Collins)

Early morning preparations before the morning meeting

Morning prayer in Fort Collins, Colorado (Photo courtesy of Karen Collins)

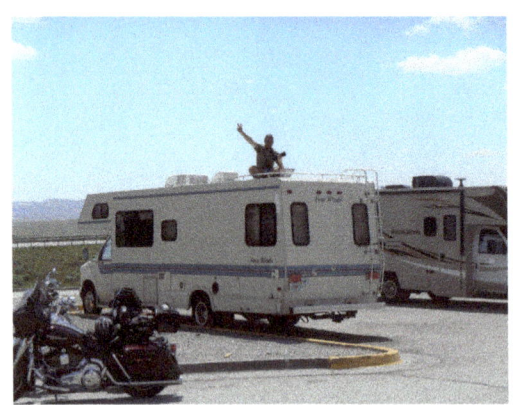

Friendly photographer atop his camper

The bag of stuff I shipped home from Idaho Falls, Idaho

The young ladies who shared their puppies with us

Momma Bear is interviewed by a TV crew in Ogden, Utah

In West Yellowstone, Montana, we split into two groups, and the second group waited ten minutes before leaving. The Ride Captains and Jeff share a laugh while we wait.

The beautiful, relaxing ride to Bozeman, Montana (Photo courtesy of Karen Collins)

Left to right - Elaine, our sweep, myself, and Karen (Ghost), my roommate (Photo courtesy of Diane Stupalski)

Morning lineup in Billings, Montana

The group at Devil's Tower, northeast Wyoming

The patch for the ride. For each year of participation, a new rocker patch is earned.

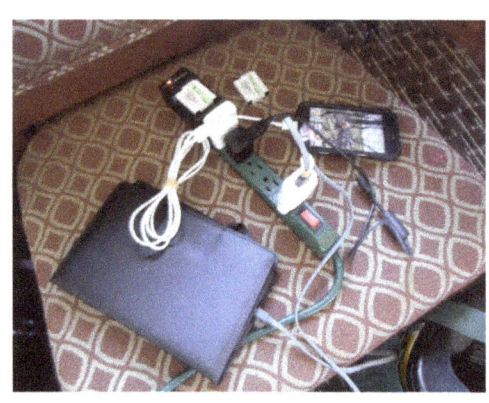

Charging all the things in the hotel room each night

A proper "chap pack" (Full chaps folded into a small pack to conserve space.)

Some of the beautiful architecture in Deadwood, South Dakota

Aric, the state trooper we made friends with at a South Dakota gas stop (Photo courtesy Karen Collins)

A very early, cold morning as we pack our bikes in the parking ramp outside our hotel in Deadwood, South Dakota

Another future rider whose family approached us at a gas stop

The trophy my sister bestowed on me upon arriving in Milwaukee, Wisconsin

A selfie the last morning of the ride. Thinking, "This is what a biker looks like!"

Bike Night at the Harley-Davidson Museum in Milwaukee, Wisconsin

Karen and a handful of riders from the ride present the funds that will provide service dogs for several veterans
(Photo courtesy of Karen Collins)

The organizer of the ride and everyone's favorite lady, Karen "Momma Bear" Collins
(Photo courtesy of Karen Collins)

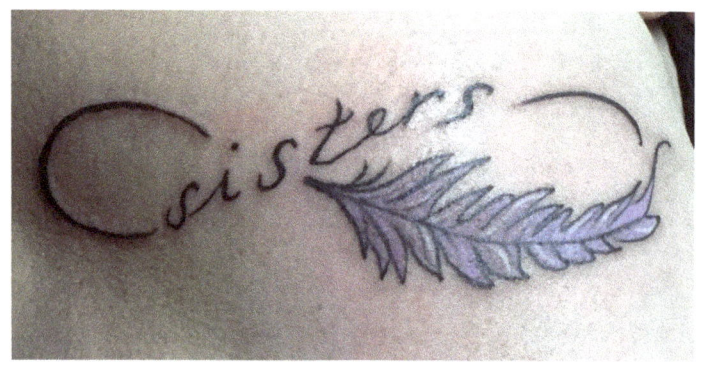

Official Tattoo of the 2017 Women's Freedom Ride
(Photo courtesy of Jean Everly)

GAG REEL

Untimely shot while gassing up on a practice run—never trust the GoPro

Never be afraid to wear pigtails on your helmet

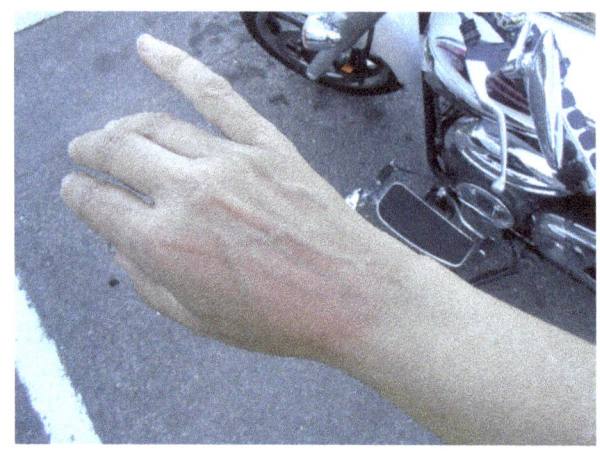

Don't forget to actually wear the sunscreen you brought!

Momma Bear having some fun with Jeffrey, our support guy

The very appropriate ice cream treat I chose after fighting the winds in Wyoming for several hours

The ice cream shop in Deadwood was so busy, this police officer stepped in to help!

My roommates Annette and Diane showing off their booties

My best buddy on the ride Karen (Ghost) mugs for the camera at a Denny's in Mauston, Wisconsin

One of the riders from Minnesota sporting a purple tutu

Angela, Diane, and myself in a light-hearted moment
(Photo courtesy of Diane Stupalski)

This is how tough biker girls have a little fun
(Photo courtesy of Diane Stupalski)

Biker Girl Meltdowns and Racing against the Storm

Tuesday, June 6
Blue Springs, Missouri, to Hays, Kansas

The ladies typically wake up about three hours before "kickstands up." I'm not a morning person, so I was always the last one out of bed and out of the room. The general pattern was to get packed up, get the stuff on the bike, make sure the bike was gassed up, and then head over for breakfast and relax for a bit.

But today I was running late. I had gone down to the bike to load up, and when I came back to the room to get the rest of my things, my key wouldn't work. Getting another key set me back with time, and I figured I would grab something quick or just skip breakfast.

As I was packing my bike, a voice came from the backseat of the car parked beside me. A sleepy face peered out the window - a young woman's - and she inquired about all the motorcycles. When I told her who we were and what we were riding for, her response was pretty amusing.

"All women?! ALL RIGHT!" It made me smile.

To make things worse, there were also posters to sign. The group had posters made with photos of us with our bikes, and we were going to hand them out at the Colmery-O'Neil VA Medical

Center in Topeka that afternoon. When I got to the breakfast area, I noticed a handful of other riders still getting breakfast, along with Jeff, who drove the support vehicle, so I did too. What I didn't know was that the ride leaders were antsy to get going, and most everyone had already lined up in the parking lot.

I was the first of the late breakfast group out to the parking lot, and got an earful from the ride captains.

"What's going on? Where is everybody??" They hollered at me angrily.

"Everyone's still eating breakfast, including Jeff, and some are still signing posters!" I responded.

"Well what the heck?! Tell them we need to get on the road if we want to miss the heavy traffic ahead!" the captains yelled to me across the group of bikes, lined up side by side in preparation for departure.

I went back inside to relay the message and then hurried back out to my bike to make sure everything was secure. We held the morning briefing quickly. We were headed into Topeka's early morning rush hour traffic and would split into two groups, 10 minutes apart, to navigate more easily.

Many times, the morning briefing would paint the day more treacherous than it ended up being. Today was not one of those days, though. Topeka has many rolling, curving hills, and seeing ahead for any distance is difficult. We'd be rolling through at 75 mph, which didn't make it a relaxing ride. I was tense, since keeping the required formation distance was now much more difficult. Two seconds behind the rider in front of me, and one second behind the rider to my left, not to mention I had to keep an eye on the traffic around me, which could at any time move into our line without notice.

A little bit about riding formation: Once on the highway, the group rides together in the left lane. This keeps us from having to worry about traffic coming onto the highway from the on-ramps and moving over each time. When traffic needs to pass the group, which many times stretched out over a mile, they do so in the right lane. It works very well, until someone in a car who doesn't have a clue comes along. Or until traffic builds up behind a slower semi-truck in the right lane, and then all sorts of things can go wrong.

When you see a group of motorcycle riders on the highway, their behavior is all about keeping themselves safe. We are much safer together than we are split, or as single riders. We want to keep the group together, and if a vehicle interrupts the line, the group is going to be stressed until that "hole" is healed. Many times a vehicle would simply pull into our line in the left lane, pass a semi, and move back into the right lane. That's how it's supposed to work. Drivers pull up behind the semi, put their turn signal on, make eye contact with the riders, wait for the "go ahead" sign, and proceed.

That's the polite way to do it, anyway. If you're on the highway and moving past motorcyclists, please be aware that as you ride along in your quiet, windless vehicle safe from the elements, looking at your phone or having a conversation with others in the vehicle, the motorcyclist you are passing is in another world, completely focused on the road conditions—the weather, the wind, the sky, every vehicle around them, and the distance between those vehicles—and is quite vulnerable because of all these factors. Especially so if the drivers nearby are on their cell phones.

If anything goes wrong, the cyclist has the most to lose. As a responsible driver, you are wise to pay full attention, and make sure you take measures to give cyclists enough space to react should something go awry. At times, vehicles would pull into our line and never leave, as we were cruising along at the speed limit or just over. But this is a mistake, making it difficult for the cyclists in back to see around and know what the cyclists in front are doing.

Are there road hazards? Is there a big gap? Roadkill or debris? It's a little bump for you in the car, but it could mean the end of the day's ride and a hospital stay for us. At this point, a ride captain would pull out of the line, ride up to that vehicle, and direct it out of the line, and not in a particularly ladylike way. It was one of my favorite times on the ride, to see angry road captains signaling the errant driver with large, intimidating arm movements and loud voices to get back into their lane. Yep, you don't mess with our line.

As we rode on, we watched two storm cells close in on our destination for the evening, and we were racing to get there before they collided. It was going to be close.

When there is a road hazard, it's customary to point it out to the riders behind you. You can use your hands or your feet for this, but most used their feet to point out problems on the road, as generally your feet are always less busy. The only the problem with that is that at high speeds, there are high winds, and the winds can really yank on any appendage you put out there.

After a few days of nervous, high-focus riding, I found I had been gripping the tank with my legs and my groin muscle was sad and sore about that. I put out my right leg to signal a pothole and cried out at the pain caused by the wind whipping it back. Oh, well, I thought, the hazards on my right are going to remain a mystery to the riders behind me for today, or until this muscle heals.

We arrived at the Colmery-O'Neil VA Medical Center to a happy welcoming group and lined up our bikes all pretty in the parking lot. We were quietly told that if we were "packing," to lock it up. I had only brought a little kayak knife, but that, too, had to be secured. The staff at the medical center was concerned that any weapons carried by the women of the ride might fall into the wrong hands, so we were asked to secure them properly in order to alleviate the risk of an incident. My bags didn't lock, so the woman parked next to me offered to store my knife in her locked bags. Later on in the week, I would ask Karen, my roommate, how many women on the ride were carrying their own gun, and she said, "Probably about half of them." So there was good reason for this preventive measure by the staff.

We were given refreshments outside and then escorted into the building, where, after a short wait, we had the opportunity to meet a small gathering of veterans and chat with them for a while. We had been told to keep things low key and quiet, be mindful of their experience, and not to ask directly, but allow them to lead the conversation and just to listen supportively, and thank them for their service. A shy, quiet group, they seemed happy for the visit, appreciated the posters, and posed for photos with us. It was a lovely time with them.

It was a warm day, and after our visit at the medical center, we were escorted to lunch at the Historic Harley-Davidson dealership in the same city. A local TV station interviewed "Momma Bear" with our bikes and the group in the background.

We had gotten a lot of attention on our ride, 31 women crossing the country on motorcycles. When we roared into or out of a gas station, we got used to seeing people pull out their cameras. "We've never seen so many women on motorcycles!" was something we heard often.

Later that afternoon, the day got really warm, and Kansas got ugly. The further west we rode, the fewer trees there were, and the sky became the most interesting thing to watch. As we rode on, we watched two storm cells close in on our destination for the evening, and we were racing to get there before they collided. It was going to be close.

We did make it, but I was tired from the ride, and upon getting to the hotel, made a few mistakes. I parked too far from the front door and for some reason decided to unload my bike there. Turned out the hotel room was on the complete opposite side of the hotel from the lobby, and there was no inside hallway to get there.

I got a luggage cart, but in my fatigue forgot the room number. I figured I might luck out and spot one of my three roommates unpacking their bikes and taking things into the room, but after scanning the parking lot a half dozen times, none of my roommates appeared to be in sight. At that point I decided to desert my luggage cart in a random parking space and head back to the lobby to ask for the room number, but the woman unpacking her bike next to me had issues with that, and snapped at me about it. I guess she had had a rough day on the road as well.

As I walked across the parking lot, a few other riders chided me about my poor choices, and in my bad mood, it made me feel sad and alone. These petty interactions were all I needed to put me right over the edge. After getting the room number from the hotel desk clerk, I held back the tears as I pushed the luggage cart for what seemed like a mile to the back of the hotel. Arriving at the correct room, I quickly opened the door and angrily threw my things onto the floor next to the bed.

This had happened before. I'm actually an introvert, and too many days outside my comfort zone without any private time to deal with the stress of that had pushed me into meltdown phase. It typically happens on every vacation with similar conditions—it's just a matter of when.

I had once been on an Alaskan cruise for almost a week when a breakdown hit. I had been pushed all week into a schedule that stressed me out by my then-husband, getting up earlier than I'd like, spending long hours socializing with the group we came with, and not having enough time to actually relax. I broke down at breakfast at the end of the week on Friday morning, making the meal uncomfortable for our friends. I was surprised to have kept it together so long, to be honest, but no one seemed to appreciate that.

It's not a good idea to deny me my down time. It happened again years later when I went to Mexico with a friend. After a week of running all over Puerto Vallarta and the surrounding area in buses and taxis and socializing all day for a series of days, not to mention the language barrier stress, it was a Friday again when that meltdown occurred. I don't think we spoke to each other that whole day, at the airport, or on the plane on the way home. I guess I should keep my vacations short, or go alone.

I knew it was going to happen sometime, and I hadn't planned on it happening quite so early on this ride, but it had been a long day, and I was worn down. I just needed some quiet time, and I would be fine.

My roommates sensed something was wrong and tried to find out what had made me so upset. They asked questions and made some guesses, but I wasn't talking. I knew if I talked about it at that moment, I would just become more upset and it would seem a bigger deal than it was, and I didn't want that. Plus, I knew if I kept the conversation short that they would leave me alone sooner, and that was my goal.

I knew everyone would soon be off to dinner and I could have the room to myself for a while, and I really needed that. I just needed to wait it out. Outside the storm had finally hit, and it was a good one. I love storms, and it was actually cheering me up. Problem was, the group was to have dinner at the local Harley-Davidson dealer, and no one wanted to ride over in the storm, so in an awesome effort of generosity, the dealer brought the meal to us, and the thankful group ate in the hotel lobby.

I stayed back to enjoy the quiet, and the storm. Once alone, I had a good cry in the shower and felt a lot better. My roommates returned after supper, I explained what happened, and we all had a good laugh at the day's misfortunes and my meltdown. We spent the evening sharing funny moments from the day, enjoying a drop-in visit from another rider, and laughing pretty hard at the raw jokes about pull-start vibrators that biker girls like to tell.

A New Perspective on Traffic, Mountains, and Wind

Wednesday, June 7
Hays, Kansas, to Fort Collins, Colorado

In the morning, we had breakfast in the lobby's large seating area. Diane, one of my roommates, was telling funny, loud stories that were, um . . . a little off color. The ladies can be loud at times, and are never apologetic about it. I was very entertained watching the handful of truckers eating breakfast, doing their best to pretend to be watching the television and ignoring our intense "girl talk." A couple with young children came into the lobby and looked around nervously. They quickly got their food and headed back out to the parking lot, where I think they ended up eating their meal. Probably a good idea, as the kids would have learned a few new words from us.

I found it especially amusing, since most of us were mothers and grandmothers ourselves. One of the riders who must've rethought the previous day's events took a moment to apologize for her snapping at me, and although I appreciated that deeply, I made light of it and told her not to worry about it. It was good to know that biker girls care about hurt feelings. Outside, while we waited for the bikes to line up, a gentleman chatted me up.

"So what are you ladies up to this morning?"

"This is the Women's Freedom Ride. It's a women's-only ride, and we're riding to generate donations for disabled veterans. This year we're trying to raise $21,000 toward training service dogs for several disabled vets."

"Wow, that's cool. So where are you headed?"

"Well, the ride begins and ends in Charleston, South Carolina, and every year the route is different. This year we're headed west to Fort Collins, Wyoming, Idaho, and then coming back through the northern states. I'll be with them until they hit Milwaukee, then I'll be heading home, since I live in central Wisconsin."

"Wow! That's a long ride. How long will it take?"

"19 states in 18 days. We're on day five."

"That's awesome! Can I donate?"

"Sure, that would be great! Thanks!"

And that was typically how most of the conversations would go.

This was a common occurrence, not only in the mornings but anytime we gathered—at a gas stop, at lunch, or as we unpacked our bikes at the end of the day. It was fun to engage strangers this way, and many times it resulted in a donation.

New people would join any time of day: during our morning meeting, a gas or lunch stop, or in the evenings at our hotel. They would be introduced, and then we would review the hand signals with the group, so the new riders would know what to look for, and how to signal it. When new people joined the ride, you'd notice things. They'd typically do a lot of braking and other odd riding behavior as they assimilated to riding in formation. I realized I was that way as well on my first few days, so I took it in stride, just being extra wary of the situation on the road in case the newbies were too concerned with their own ride to notice.

When you're on a bike, you have only a moment to identify the problem and react, and you want as much warning of that problem as you can possibly develop. Your eyes, ears, and body are constantly monitoring for changes. Sudden changes are your first clue, and many times your only clue, so you pay close attention to them.

That morning, as we rode down the highway, everything seemed to be going along well, when I noticed something fly off a bike about a half dozen riders ahead of me. I had about a half second to determine if it was hard or soft, and if I needed to take evasive action. The item fell to the pavement and exploded, shattering bright silver fragments in all directions. By the time I passed it, it was no longer a hazard. At the next stop, we discovered it had been Anja's mirror, shaken loose from the vibration of her bike. The worse part? Her GoPro had been attached to it, and now it was lost forever.

It was annoying to see so many motorists on their phones and not focused on traffic. In a car it might seem unimportant, but to a motorcyclist it can mean life and death. Many times cars would cut into our line without any warning, misinterpreting our staggered formation as an opening for a lane change. I found myself reacting to this by narrowing these spaces when I became aware of a car wanting to change lanes to pass a semi. I felt we were safer together, and that the car should wait for the entire group to pass before making the attempt.

However, another lady on the ride had other ideas and instead would open the gap and wave the car into our lane. Sometimes the driver would understand and take the opportunity, but many times they wouldn't, and that would leave an even worse gap in our line, and it was difficult to catch up with the rest of the group.

I found this upsetting, so when we would get to a gas stop, I made sure I was in front of that motorcyclist as we lined up to leave, so I wouldn't have to deal with it. By doing so, I realized that the closer one rode to the front of the line, the less problems there were with the "slinky" effect.

One day I found myself directly behind the ride captains, and it was like heaven. There were no gaps, no catching up, no cars cutting into our line, and no missed communication. Occasionally the captains would use hand signals to indicate a situation ahead, and these signals would be passed down the line to the rest of the riders. Only when I rode in the front did I realize how many of these signals were "lost in translation," as not all the riders were efficient with passing them along.

So, Who Are the Women of the Women's Freedom Ride?

I haven't written much yet about the amazing women of the ride. I think it's best to say—whatever you think about biker girls, you're wrong. We're just ladies who like to ride bikes. Sure, some are loud, but many are not. Sure, some act cocky, but many are shy. Sure, some act fearless, but many had the exact same fears I was feeling while riding down the road.

Biker girls are tough ladies and say what's on their mind, but they still worry about hurting others' feelings, and their feelings can get hurt. I had my meltdown and thought it was an anomaly, but this happened many times among the ladies in the group, and each time it was met with great support. The stress of riding 350 to 400 miles on an average day wore down some of the best riders, and it was nothing to be ashamed of.

Wednesday, June 7, was a ride day—no social stops, which was a mixed blessing. I can understand now why rock bands on tour tend to forget what day it is, and which town they're in. The days were beginning to blur, and the social stops helped break up the day between the physical and the cerebral. Today we would have less of that.

The day had blurred so much that I didn't even realize we had ridden into Colorado. The ugly flat nothing of west Kansas had simply become the ugly, slightly-less-flat nothing of eastern

Colorado. We were racing against a storm again and heading into Denver traffic, which was some of the worst on the trip. As we turned north towards Fort Collins in congested multi-lane traffic, it became even more difficult to navigate. The high number of vehicles cutting into our line badly split the group, and it was almost impossible to change lanes.

After almost a week on the road, however, what would have been a reaction of fear and avoidance had now evolved to anger and ownership, and I found myself aggressively reprimanding a guy in a pickup truck for not allowing me to move over.

> *"How many women do you guess on this ride are packing a gun?" I asked.*

I needed to switch lanes to catch up to the group. I put on my turn signal and checked over my left shoulder to find two men in a white pickup truck just off my rear left side. I sped up a bit, and checked the lane again. The pickup was in the exact same place, so I sped up again. Looking over my shoulder to check for what I thought would be one last time, I found the white pickup again in the exact same spot. I realized the guys were messing with me, but in this situation it was anything but amusing. This was a dangerous game, and I could lose my life trying to win.

I felt rage surge up inside me. I looked the driver dead in the eye and gestured strongly with my arm, pointing at myself, and then the lane beside me. I knew he couldn't hear me or read my lips in the full-face helmet I was wearing, but I said, "I'M GOING HERE. NOW." With everything I had, and I meant it. I rolled back on the throttle, and before he could react, I changed lanes in a very slim window of opportunity, and sped away. I wanted to get away from that "yo-yo" as my dad would have put it, as fast as I could.

Wow, who was this woman? I thought, with a mix of pride and amusement and I rolled down the highway towards the storm clouds looming over Fort Collins, and the rest of the group.

Safely at the hotel while unpacking, the group was boisterous, releasing stress from the day, when we noticed a little girl watching us from the veranda of the hotel with her grandmother. Both were smiling, and eventually the girl was invited to come down and pose for a photo while sitting on one of the bikes. The ride is all about empowering and encouraging women riders, and this is how they start. We were happy to oblige.

That evening, after a fun supper with the ride captains at an open-air restaurant just down the street, some ladies decided to do their laundry, and several chose to wash their bikes. My roommate Karen and I hung out in the room and chatted about things, which was becoming a nightly routine. Our roommates Diane and Annette would be out socializing, so we always had some time in the room on our own to share and rant about the day's events. I looked forward to these moments, when I could speak freely and ask dumb questions about things that were on my mind.

This night, after Karen grabbed us a Coke and a snack, we sat together on the bed in the hotel room, and I decided to ask her about the weapons we were asked to secure.

"How many women do you guess on this ride are packing a gun?" I asked.

"Oh, at least half of 'em." Karen replied.

Karen walked over to her luggage and pulled out a small

black bag and tossed it onto the bed in front of me, gesturing for me to open it up and take a look.

It was a small handgun, a Ruger 9. I'd had a little experience with guns and shooting them, but not much. Karen was a military veteran, and so she was pretty comfortable with carrying a piece. I wasn't so sure I was ready for that, but I felt very safe knowing that if we were on the road and things went to hell, that over a dozen women would be there to take control of the situation. I felt a little silly for just having a kayak knife along, but I hadn't taken it as a means of self-defense. That's what the pepper spray was for. Sometimes you just need a knife, and it's good to have one handy.

We spent the rest of the evening chatting about family stuff and whatnot. It had been a really warm day on the bikes, and after a nice cool shower to refresh ourselves, the coolness of the air conditioning in the room was dearly welcome and comforting, as were the soft drinks and candy we were enjoying.

Thursday, June 8
Fort Collins, Colorado, to Rock Springs, Wyoming

In the morning, we got into a little trouble. Someone put a little music on, and we all got happy dancing in the parking lot. Unfortunately, it was about 5:30 a.m., and one of the hotel residents must have complained about it, because the manager told us to shut it down. Someone had put the kibosh on our activity. What, isn't everyone up at this hour? I bet the two dozen Harleys firing up about a half hour later bothered them even more.

Another activity I enjoyed were the little gifts the riders

shared with each other. Sabrina, one of the ride captains, surprised me by buying my gas at a gas stop, so I later bought her lunch. Many of us showed our appreciation to the ride organizers and captains by purchasing their meals and other little perks and treats along the way. Every night, just after checking in, my roommate, Karen, would get herself a Diet Coke and bring me a regular one as well. I must have owed her about a dozen, but she'd never let me pay her back.

By the way, we had three Karens on the ride, which as you can imagine got a little confusing. There was the ride leader Karen, "Momma Bear," and Karen was also the name of one of the ride captains (we referred to her as "Karen 2.0"), and my roommate Karen, whose nickname was "Ghost," because she rode a pale grey Yamaha.

We used nicknames almost exclusively, which caused a problem for me. When I received a donation one morning before we rode off, I asked who to give the money to, as I didn't know who was officially collecting the donations. "Carol" the answer came back, and having ridden at that point for over a week and not knowing who that was, I spouted, "Carol?! Who the hell is Carol?" Well, I knew her as "Tink," because Carol wears bells on her belt loops. I had no idea what her real name was!

Thursday morning, after climbing a few mountains and battling through strong winds, our refreshment stop was at High Country Motorsports of Cheyenne in Wyoming. A beauty pageant winner, Mrs. Wyoming, was there to greet us and chat, and pose for a photo op. A few bikes had minor problems that needed fixing, so I used the time to chat up Jill and Wendy, two new riders who had joined us. We had a great conversation, and chatted about how they had started a women's riding group in the Denver area. Unfortunately, they weren't with us for more than a day, and left the ride. I guessed the intensity of the ride was more than they expected and wanted to deal with. It happens.

Lunch at a truck stop in Rawlins, Wyoming, was a good time. A gentleman perched atop a large camper took photos as we came and went from our bikes, so I took his right back. Two young ladies on a cross-country trip of their own were curious about us and shared their puppies with the group, many of whom badly needed a puppy fix, having been gone from their own pups for a week now. It was fun to see a group of "tough biker girls" get all googly eyed and cooing over the dogs, and I didn't miss the opportunity to razz them about it. Amidst all the fuss over the dogs, I noticed Momma heading quietly to her bike and backing it out, a sign that fun time was over, and it was time to ride. Not wanting to be the last one ready, I thanked the girls, wished them well on their trip home, and headed over to my bike. As we lined up to go, people in the parking lot grabbed their cameras to record the spectacle.

> *It took literally everything I had physically and emotionally to stay the course for those 103 miles.*

What we didn't know, however, was that the worst part of the trip was yet to come. On our way to Rock Springs, Wyoming, our stop for the night, we had to travel through what I considered hell: a road down to two lanes due to road construction. In road construction areas, the group rides in single file for safety. Late afternoon, as the sun was going down, all I could see were silhouettes of the bikers in front of me, save for their taillights. The center of the road was divided with tall, stick-type pylons, and on my left was an oncoming lane crowded with semis hurtling toward me at 85 mph.

That's right, the speed limit in Wyoming is 80, so five over is what most drive at. On my right was a deep ditch. Why did I notice the ditch? Because at that time of day, the conditions are just right to create 40 mph wind gusts that come at you from both directions. I spent 103 miles counter-steering into those gusts, brutally battering us from one side and the other without warning.

I fought as hard as I could just to stay in my own lane. I was terrified that I would overcorrect at some point and end up in the ditch, or worse . . . like a fly on the windshield of an oncoming semi. In motorcycle riding, there's a simple rule to avoid an accident: Look where you want to go. So I decided to ignore the ditch on my right and the semis on my left and focus on those taillights in front of me. I figured if the rest of the girls were out here doing this, it must be doable, and I could do it, too.

It took literally everything I had physically and emotionally to stay the course for those 103 miles. I can't tell you how happy I was to see the exit for Rock Springs and the parking lot of our hotel. When my bike finally rolled to a stop, I laid my head on the tank in exhaustion and disbelief.

It was Ghost's birthday that day, and our roommates Diane, Annette, and Diane's friend Angela brought gifts of soda and cupcakes to the room, sang the birthday song to Karen, and left after an oddly brief visit. Ghost and I laughed about that, and hung out in the room that evening. It was a beautiful room with brand-new furnishings and a bathroom the size of a small apartment.

After enjoying a nice long hot shower, we sat and bitched about everything we loved and hated about the ride.

That evening there was a gorgeous full moon hanging low in the Wyoming night sky, and I felt it was a well-earned gift for the pains I had endured that day on the road.

Commandeering the Local IHOP, Bike Drops at Gas Stops, and a Day Off

Friday, June 9
Rock Springs, Wyoming, to Idaho Falls, Idaho

In the morning, as I stepped off the elevator with my bags, I heard someone in the lobby mention that there was no breakfast at our hotel. Well, there was, if you wanted to purchase one and stick it in the microwave for a few minutes.

Pity, since the room was marvelous, complete with a full kitchen and full-size refrigerator. Too bad we weren't staying another night, as it was one of the nicer rooms on the trip. Ghost and I had our bikes packed and ready before most, so we went to get gas. Someone had mentioned there was an IHOP down the road, and we planned on heading over after gassing up.

Almost as beautiful as the moon the night before was the amazing sunrise that greeting us in the morning, almost like an apology for the terrifying ride the day before. Apology accepted! Ghost and I were in a great mood, and were shouting back and forth across the pumps as we filled up our respective tanks. As we pulled out, Ghost was in front of me and almost pulled into the path of a large truck, but spotted it at the last moment. My heart just about stopped then, and I was reminded just how vulnerable we are at the times you least expect. You can't let your guard down at any moment when you're on a motorcycle—there's just too much at risk.

When we walked in to the restaurant, the waitress, the only one there, smiled and said, "For two?" and we replied, "Ah, no... more like 30." Her eyes got real big, and I said, "Don't worry, we'll help you. But you should call in some additional help." We proceeded to set the tables in the back area with napkins, utensils, coffee cups, and menus. We ordered right away and explained the situation to our girls as they showed up, a few at a time.

Some, upon hearing the bad news, decided to head down the street to McDonald's to help ease the burden. The restaurants' regulars also came streaming in, and it became clear that even a second waitress was not going to be much help. It was at that point my roommate Diane decided to commandeer the kitchen.

As she brought out plates of food, she would holler out the order and ask who had what. Others brought out coffee to the girls. It was quite a scene, but it was working well. The waitresses were free to handle the regulars, and we got our food. When I apologized for the chaos to one of the waitresses, she said, "You guys are GREAT!"

Too bad we couldn't stay to help clean up . . . but we do tip well.

We ended up having the morning briefing right there inside the IHOP. I was teased mercilessly by the group and called a "pussy" with a "scared vagina" by several for admitting my fear from our ride in the day prior, but even the teasing made me feel like I'd earned a badge of honor, and their respect.

Once on the road, the scenery was beautiful: big, red hills, curves, and snow-capped mountains. I dared to look away from the road now and then, but not for long, since things could change quickly on the road in front of me. Some ladies had their cameras at the end of a lanyard around their neck and would hold them out in the general direction of the scenery and snap photos without looking, later deleting the bad ones. I didn't feel comfortable riding one-handed at 85 mph, so I only took photos while standing still.

We arrived at the Golden Spike Harley-Davidson in Ogden, Utah, for lunch. As usual, the ladies dismounted and dispersed throughout the dealership, some seeking a shopping experience, while others hit the ladies room for relief. This being my first trip over three hours long, I had been forming a list of needs for safety and comfort. At this point my list read: locking bags and yellow lenses. I didn't know much about what sort of yellow lenses I needed, so I approached one of the road captains, Karen 2.0. Karen 2.0 didn't smile much, which seemed to be a common thread among the road captains.

I had kept my distance long enough and finally felt sure enough to bother her with a question, so I asked her about her yellow lensed glasses as we were walking around the store. She was more than helpful with her response, very supportive and offered advice and suggestions for a myriad of other items I was curious about. Her enthusiastic response made me feel validated. I scolded myself internally for being too shy to approach her or any of the other ride captains sooner. I was still on a learning curve and feeling my way with this group on some levels, but shyness was going to get me absolutely nowhere. What was I afraid of? I realized I needed to relax and just flow with it, and be sure of myself.

The lunch we enjoyed that day was one of the best on the

ride, as we were served box lunches with fresh sandwiches, a bag of chips, and a pickle, complete with soft, delicious cookies for dessert. Our fearless leader, "Momma Bear," was interviewed by local television, and the TV crew put together a great video of our time there, including a shot of us heading out to our next destination, which they posted on Facebook.

The group rolled out feeling good, inside and out. However, it was one of the longer days on the bike, and as the day wore on, it also wore us out. The road captains had told us during the morning meeting that it would be a long day of riding, so we would keep the gas stops very short. Typically we'd have a good 45 minutes to gas up, use the bathroom, relax, and grab a snack, but they wanted us in and out and back on the road today, so we had that added pressure as well.

Sometimes fatigue sneaks up on you, and it got to a few of us that afternoon. At one gas stop, Anja dropped her bike as she was pulling up to the pump. I gasped inside my helmet, because it was one of the bigger bikes on the ride, a beautiful copper-colored Kawasaki Vulcan painted with flames. The sight of it lying on its side made me want to cry. I can only imagine how Anja felt.

Of course, a half dozen girls immediately swarmed the bike to help pick it up, and all was well. But at the next gas stop, another woman dropped her bike, and in my own rush to fill my tank, I spilled gasoline all over the bike, and panicked. I called a road captain over to ask her what to do about it. She thought I was trying to be funny, so she barked at me loudly and told me to stop goofing off. That didn't help my panic, and when I explained I was worried about the spill catching fire on a hot bike, she changed her tone and told me it wasn't a concern.

I was starting to wonder if we were being pushed a little too hard that day—but it wasn't my call, and we kept moving on down the road. Of course, there were light-hearted moments that day, like the gas stop where we took the opportunity to dance for a bit and let off a little steam.

Then there was another where I was returning from the ladies' room to discover Becky, a rider from Nebraska, surrounded by Japanese tourists who wanted a photo with her. She had said yes to one of them, and that was all it took. I laughed and figured we'd be at this station for longer than we thought. She seemed to be enjoying herself, so I didn't rescue her. In fact, I slinked away quickly, lest I get caught up in the madness as well.

"If you got this far and haven't fallen over yet, you're doin' good!"

With a bit of luck, we beat the rain again as we rolled into our hotel in Idaho Falls, Idaho. We'd be in town for two days, so the girls decided to unwind a bit at Jaker's, a great restaurant across the street. It was a fun evening filled with funny stories, love, and laughter. We even got a donation from Jaker's and a photo op with the manager.

At one point, I received a high compliment from Angela, one of the more experienced riders. We had been chatting at the table after dinner about the ride so far, and to my complete surprise, Angela paused to tell me that I was doing really well. The more experienced riders and ride captains mostly keep to themselves, and I didn't seek out their attention out of respect, and not wanting to be an annoying newbie, so this was an unexpected moment for me.

"Really??" I spurted.

"Oh yeah," she said. "If you got this far and haven't fallen over yet, you're doin' good!"

I was beaming for the rest of the night: 364 miles for the day, 2,445 since I'd left home.

The next morning the breakfast area had been taken over by those Japanese tourists I mentioned earlier, and they were cleaning out supplies faster than the help could restock. As we watched the carnage, the ladies tossed around ideas for what to do that day; many were headed to Yellowstone National Park to see the sights. The problem was, Yellowstone was almost two full hours away, one way. Add in traffic, the visit at the park, and the return trip, and you have a whole day of riding. I wanted a day off from riding down the highway at breakneck speed, so I planned to spend the day enjoying the city.

My roommate Ghost said she was thinking the same thing, and we decided to spend the day together. Our roommates had noticed our growing friendship over the past few days and often teased us about being a couple. I didn't mind. Ghost and I had shared quite a few conversations alone in the hotel rooms, and found that we had a lot in common, one of which was that we both were empaths, and struggled with the same issues due to that.

Empaths are people who have a deep sense of what others around them are feeling, and feel those emotions as if they were their own. An empath has so much empathy, they literally take on other's people's feelings, like a sponge. They don't just feel sad for someone, they actually feel the sadness they are feeling. This happens with any emotion, and when it is a group of people feeling the same emotion, it can be overwhelming, and sometime debilitating.

Not many people understand that, but when Ghost and I connected on that point, she shared a few tricks that she had learned about protecting herself in that situation, and I immediately put them into practice. I was glad to find that kinship with her, and it grew with each day we were on the ride.

I was thrilled to have the company that day. We started by heading over to the local FedEx to ship some things home. I had a 15-pound bag of stuff I no longer needed for the ride.

Half the ride was over, and I had found myself using the same clothing items again and again. I had packed extra clothing, but gotten very efficient at layering and reading the weather for the day's riding, and no longer needed it. When packing I wasn't sure how much time I would have to wash clothes on the ride, but as it happened, one of my roommates did laundry every few days and would gladly wash everyone else's along with hers. There was no need to haul the extra stuff, since it was just excess weight on the bike that I didn't need.

When Ghost and I arrived at FedEx, we ran into Elaine, another rider sending home her dirty laundry. Apparently this lucky lady had a husband at home who would have it all washed and put away by the time she returned home.

Ghost rode a Yamaha V-Star just a year older than mine, and she and I, weary of visiting Harley dealerships for days, decided to visit the local Yamaha dealer. The contrast was amusing. The guys there were great, but it was clear the shop had been converted from a spacious, smelly old garage.

It reminded me of the old DX station on the corner near my high school at home that a friend of my dad's used to run. In fact, the clothes for sale on the racks and other displays actually seemed a little out of place because of the vastness and darkness of the old garage. The smell of thousands of oil changes still hung in the air, and the many scuffs and stains on the cement floor bore witness to the history of all the repair work that had occurred in that space over the last six or seven decades. I found the juxtaposition quite amusing and found myself smiling.

Harley dealerships are typically spotless, shiny, and colorful, and this shop was . . . not. I felt good about it though, figuring that Yamaha wasn't overcharging us for bikes or accessories. Harley riders often joke that HD stands for another "Hundred Dollars" and the prices I saw at those stores made me believe it must certainly be true.

We spent the afternoon exploring and shopping before having a leisurely lunch at a quirky little place next to our hotel called the Bee's Knees. It felt amazing not to be rushing to get someplace and to have the luxury of time to ourselves.

Afterwards, Ghost took a nap and I relaxed in the hotel's hot tub all by myself, soothing my sore tailbone muscles.

It was a question I got often from the half dozen people I kept in touch with during the ride via phone. "Be honest . . . how does your butt feel?" And most of the time, most days, it felt fine. The gas stops really helped. I found that as we neared each one, though, my bottom would start to ache, and so I would try different sitting positions to alleviate the pain.

Pushing one hip forward and then the other worked well, as did butt crunches. Occasionally I'd have to stand up once we got to a stop sign to get some temporary relief. There weren't many. I joked with the ride leaders that they should work on acquiring massage therapists as sponsors. A lot of ladies agreed with me on that one. A little shoulder massage right after lunch would have been the bomb.

Speaking of stop signs, something I haven't mentioned yet is one of the coolest things on the ride. When we needed to move the group through an intersection, the ride captains would block traffic in each direction so that the group could move forward as a unit safely. It's not exactly legal, but it did keep the riders safe. Occasionally, someone in a car would refuse to stop or get ornery about it. If ignoring them while standing our ground didn't work, we simply worked around it, and continued once the intersection was clear again. I must admit, I loved breaking the rules and riding through stoplights when we did this. It really makes you feel like a VIP.

Cold Mornings, Bad Hotels, and a Very Special Dinner Guest

Sunday, June 11
Idaho Falls, Idaho, to Billings, Montana

We woke up to a cold, windy, 54-degree morning.

Most ladies were from the south, and cold for them is defined a little differently than those of us who dwell in the northern climes. When they would complain about "cold" mornings, I would laugh at them and ride with my jacket wide open, enjoying the cool breeze. Not this morning.

On a bike, it's roughly 20 degrees colder with the wind chill. According to the chart, which only goes up to 65 mph, it's 33 degrees at that speed . . . and we would be barreling down the highway at 85. One thing about dressing for the day: you have one chance to figure out what to wear, because if you're wrong, you're screwed for the next two hours, since the group doesn't stop until we need gas.

So best to overdo it instead of risking the chance of being very cold, very warm, or very wet for several hours. Of course, you can stop, but then you'll have to catch up, and the group is riding along at 85 mph, so you do the math. I wore half of what was in my duffel bag: a pair of Under Armour leggings, two pair of socks, jeans, leather chaps, and rain pants—and that was just the bottom half.

Even when it's not raining, rain gear is excellent for keeping warm, since it does a great job of keeping the wind out as well. Despite the cold, the ride that morning turned out to be a beautiful, relaxing ride to and through the mountains. For most of the ride, we had been on four-lane highways and needed to be painfully aware of traffic merging in and out for most of our day. However, the ride through the mountains was on a two-lane road, so there could be no semis crashing past us at 85 mph, or any yo-yos trying to cut into our line.

We didn't have to worry about much, so there was space in our heads to enjoy the road, the ride, and the scenery around us. Idaho Falls had been the city furthest west on the ride, and we were now heading back east. Being a little closer to the flora and fauna brought with it a different set of dangers. At one point, I suddenly spotted a bird who flew right into our line. The wind created by our speed knocked the poor thing right into my calf. It felt like getting hit with a fastball, but there was nothing I could do about it. The riders behind me reported seeing a bouncing bird on the pavement. Poor little guy.

We stopped for gas in West Yellowstone, Montana, and broke into two groups, spaced 10 minutes apart, to better navigate the mountains ahead of us. The day was warming up, so we adjusted clothing accordingly. The ride on the way to Bozeman was even prettier than the first segment that morning, since we were now following a mountain stream that ran along the highway. Each curve brought another beautiful view of the terrain.

Perhaps too beautiful, as it became apparent that some of us were having a tough time staying alert without having to dodge all those semi trucks.

The vibration of a bike can lull you to sleep, even as you're tearing down the road at 85 mph. Things are pretty consistent on the road with a group of riders—the smells, the sounds, the pattern of bikes, so when something does change, it gets your attention. I'd learned to watch for riders having a hard time staying in the line and starting to weave just a bit, or struggle to keep the correct spacing with the bike in front of them. There wasn't much I could do but hope they were aware of it and trying to find a way to stay alert.

When we stopped in Bozeman for lunch, it was a welcome relief for those who needed the break. As we pulled into the restaurant parking lot for lunch, I noticed a rider pull to the far end of the lot. I knew that trick, and I knew what it meant. I followed her, and parked my bike near to hers. I chatted her up in an attempt to find out what was bothering her, and to my surprise she blurted out, "I can't stay awake!" and began to cry.

I felt so bad for her, because we had all been there. Trying everything you know to stay awake with none of it working is a terrifying feeling, because it's not just you that will go down if you fail, you're likely to take out a few other riders with you as well, and that sense of responsibility is probably the heaviest burden of the ride. I felt her terror, and tried to comfort her as best I could without calling more attention to it. I knew she didn't want the other girls to realize what was going on. After a few minutes of conversation she seemed all right, so I left her alone so she could collect herself.

As the girls filtered into the restaurant, the crowd responded with a lot of whispers, stares, and some smiles, as was the typical reaction at most places, and by now I was so used to it I barely noticed. After the meal, a sweet older couple chatted me up on my way out, and I was only too happy to tell them all about our cause.

I tried to point Momma out to them as she was leaving, to show them the great lady who works so hard to produce the Women's Freedom Ride year after year, but she's really good at subtly sneaking away before that can happen. I'd noticed it many times at many stops, and figured she would rather let the ladies of the ride tell the story about why we're doing this. I didn't mind at all, as people were generally very friendly and open to us when we would talk about our cause. Besides, I really wanted people to see that we were just regular people like them, and that there were many more similarities with "biker" girls than there were differences.

What always amused me was how we would accidentally "trap" people in their cars as we lined up to leave at restaurants and hotels. Focused on lining up, we'd fail to notice people sitting in their cars waiting to leave, or assumed they were just watching us out of interest. When I finally realized these people wanted to leave but were afraid to ask us to move, I started looking for this and would just walk up and ask them if they needed to leave, and then get the group to accommodate them. It amused me that we looked so intimidating that merely asking us politely to move seemed out of the question. The last thing any of us wanted was to come across as a bunch of uncooperative bullies.

That evening when we arrived in Billings, Montana, the hotel was less than satisfactory to Momma Bear. This was a first for me, and I was curious to see what was going to happen. As we all waited in the parking lot for her final word, it became apparent that the hotel had failed a quick inspection for bedbugs, so finding other accommodations was now an issue for the group.

As we were riding along, things seemed fine and stable, until I noticed a smell, and it wasn't a good one. It was the smell of over-heated metal.

Some ladies simply went to the hotel next door, or located other hotels in the area with their smart phones. A handful of us ended up at a nearby hotel that took us in at the price the lousy hotel was going to charge us. That was a big deal, because this was a brand new hotel and by far one of the nicest ones on the trip. I could have lived in that room for a month, it was so spacious and beautiful.

Later that evening, we enjoyed a dinner arranged to support a local girl who had been bullied. She had contacted Momma Bear when she heard of our ride and our cause, and we wanted to show her our support. She was a lovely young lady, and we had not only support but many gifts for her. It was a great night full of warmth, smiles, and laughter.

Monday, June 12
Billings, Montana, to Deadwood, South Dakota

Another day of horrible winds, only this day the sun was shining in the middle of a big blue sky.

It's amazing how much difference it makes in your attitude, riding when the sun is out. As we rode between the hills cut for the highway, the wind gusts also came and went accordingly. I could see the gusts smack each rider down the line as she cleared a hill, so I could tell when to brace for it. The purple mountains in the distance, although beautiful, were not much comfort. Our morning gas stop was in a lovely little valley, and

I was so happy for the break. The owner of the little local gas station was happy to see us, and not only made a donation but also posted photos of our visit to his Facebook page. It's special moments on the trip like this that made us feel like celebrities.

Unfortunately, we had to get back on the road and face that horrible wind again. It seemed worse than before, and after fighting it all morning and part of the afternoon, my neck hurt from snapping against the powerful blasts and my right arm ached from counter-steering for two hundred miles just to stay in my lane.

At our lunch stop, I pulled to the side of the lot and collapsed on the tank. I just didn't want to ride anymore. A friendly stranger walking his dog called out to me and asked if I was okay. He explained that he also rode, had been where I was, and knew how I was feeling. He talked about how brutal the wind was out there and how tough it was to be riding in it. I was grateful for that, and to know that it wasn't just me.

Only there was a slight problem. This wasn't our lunch stop, and we had some miles to go before we'd eat. Unable to cope with the thought of continuing on, I ate some crackers and had a good cry on the curb next to my bike while the group gathered on the opposite side of the lot. It was one of the handful of times I considered quitting the ride, but for what? To end up on a lonely ride home across many states on my own, without any backup?

The thought of that, and letting down all the people who supported me and donated toward the cause, made that option an impossibility. There was no way I was letting that happen. I swallowed it all up and got back on the bike and in the line.

I mentioned before about how paying attention to change

is important. As we were riding along, things seemed fine and stable, until I noticed a smell, and it wasn't a good one. It was the smell of over-heated metal.

I thought, "Okay, it has to be someone in front of me, but who?"

There was no way to tell, and I prayed a silent prayer that it wasn't going to be serious and take out a rider or several of us at once. Then I waited, and watched.

Ghost had finally got her bike repaired and running properly that morning, so she was riding with us instead of in the chase vehicle. It was a big deal, and I was happy to be riding next to her for the day. Her bike had been giving her a lot of problems, and I was starting to worry that it might happen to me, since we both rode Yamahas built only one year apart. I thought maybe the bike couldn't handle the ride, but my bike seemed to be doing all right.

Then suddenly Ghost, who was riding on my front left, lost power. I heard her curse and look down, and then lost sight of her as she fell back and pulled off. I knew Elaine, our sweep, would stop with her, and so would the chase vehicle.

I would learn later that her brake tension had fallen off, and after stopping, she went to pick up the part and burned her fingers on it. I felt so bad for Ghost and all the bad luck she'd had. But there was nothing I could do at the moment, so I focused on the road in front of me and rolled on.

Later in the day on our way to Deadwood, South Dakota, we made a stop in Wyoming at Devil's Tower, our nation's very first national monument. The ride in was amazing, along canyons of yellow rock dotted with evergreens, and looked to me just like one of those old national park postcards from the

'50s. The road was curvy and fun, and once in a while, we'd catch a glimpse of the Tower, ever closer each time.

Once there, we shopped at the trading post, enjoyed a simple lunch, and took a group photo with the famous landmark in the background. We didn't stay long, as storms were on the way, and we still had miles to go. Before we exited the parking lot, however, an older gentleman wanted to make sure we all had a tiny but free copy of the New Testament in our hands. Apparently, at least to him, we looked like we needed saving.

A Day Off in Deadwood and a Very Long Day in South Dakota

Tuesday, June 13
A Layover Day in Deadwood, South Dakota

A welcome day off. I spent too much of the morning trying hard to update the newspaper where I worked of my travels and send some photos, but I hadn't considered the problem of the hotel's glacially slow internet service.

What was even more difficult to deal with was the news of a terrible storm that had hit my hometown and that the area was devastated, and the townsfolk were struggling to deal with it. The photos on Facebook were upsetting, and knowing I was several states away and could do nothing was frustrating, to say the least.

How my co-workers even got a paper out that week was beyond me, as all of their computers were down on the two biggest production days of the week. So even if my photos had made it out, the paper wouldn't have been able to receive them.

I finally gave up on my efforts mid-morning, only to find most of the girls already off on adventures of their own in the area. We were close to a lot of interesting places such as Mount Rushmore, Crazy Horse, and Sturgis, but after the tough day on the bike the day before, I was happy just to play tourist. I wandered out of the hotel and spotted a Visitor's Center just across the street. I went in and asked where would be a good place to grab a coffee and something delicious to eat with it. The woman recommended a little gas station about a block away that had been converted into a coffee shop and art studio.

It probably couldn't have been a more perfect combination. Soon I was settled in a comfy chair in the warm sunshine, watching the world go by with a hot java and a steaming blueberry muffin in front of me, another perfect combination.

I'm the kind of person who can make conversation with anyone, and feel pretty at ease exploring a new place on my own. So after breakfast, I made my way to downtown Deadwood, a charming little town with amazing architecture and a bit of the feel of the Old West.

I wandered up and down the street, chatting with the locals and enjoying the luxury of being able to enjoy the day at my own pace. With limited storage on the bike, I'd bought very few souvenirs but managed to find a few things the grandchildren would enjoy, a few things for myself, and something for Ghost.

Ghost and I had bonded pretty deeply by this point of the ride, and I wanted to cheer her up and also show her my appreciation. But how? After perusing several shops, it struck me: a biker bell would be the perfect thing.

A biker bell is a small metal bell that is hung on the lowest part of the underside of a bike. The idea is to ward off gremlins that might cause you trouble on the road. The

I had started this ride without knowing a soul, never imagining that I'd find such a good friend, and Ghost had been there for me time after time.

story goes that the chiming of the bell causes great pain to the gremlins' ears, and will cause them to stay away. But you can't buy this bell for yourself, it must be a gift.

The bells come in just about every style you can imagine, representing all sorts of subjects to make them interesting and appealing to motorcyclists. I looked at dozens of them before deciding which one I was going to give to Ghost.

Every once in a while, I'd hear the roar of an engine come down the main street, and would look to see if it was anyone I knew, since ladies were starting to return from their rides to the nearby attractions. I ran into Ghost back at the hotel room. She'd had a rough day with repairs on her bike, so she was looking forward to having a few drinks to calm herself down.

Before we were about to leave, I told Ghost I had something for her. I dug into my bags for the bell, and held it hidden for a few moments while I told her how I felt about our new friendship.

"I was shopping today and was thinking about all these great conversations you and I have been having, and the way you're always grabbing me a Coke and a snack after we check in, and just in general how you've been helping me out on the ride, looking out for me and putting up with my crap . . . and well . . . I wanted you to have this."

I pulled out the bell and presented it to her. It was covered with hearts, which was the perfect expression of how I felt. I had started this ride without knowing a soul, never imagining that I'd find such a good friend, and Ghost had been there for me time after time.

She paused for a moment, then sprang up from her seat and ran to her luggage, digging around for a moment or two.

Then she pulled out a small pendant: a star inside a silver circle with rhinestones and little leaves scattered around the edges, attached to a small chain.

Ghost handed it to me. "I want you to have this," she said.

The moment meant a lot to both of us, and I knew if our roommates had been there, they probably would have teased us mercilessly about having a wedding ceremony. We gave each other a long hug and headed out for those drinks.

At the bar in the casino, with drinks and appetizers set before us, I was happy to listen to Ghost rant and clear her head. I wanted to help cheer her up so she could relax and enjoy the evening, and tried to crack a few jokes to lighten up her mood. It worked.

One by one the ladies came down to the bar for supper, and we eventually gathered at a long table to enjoy a meal and each other's company. Everyone was in good spirits, and there was a lot of loud laughter. We said goodbye to Glenda and Becky, two great ladies who had been riding with us for a while. It was their last night on the ride, and we were sorry to see them go.

Always friendly and ever helpful, they would definitely be missed. Glenda was from Kansas and never wore the biker black—she was always in some crazy bright color, just like her personality, and even wore pink leathers. Becky was from Nebraska, quick with a corny joke, and having run an automotive shop for many years, was always at the ready with helpful info or to clear your windshield of bugs at a gas stop. Unfortunately, I didn't realize how important that was until she left the ride.

At the end of the meal, the ride captains gave the word for "kickstands up" in the morning. It would not only be very cold, but very early as well, since it was to be our longest mileage day of the trip. Temps were expected to be around freezing at the time of departure, and nobody was excited at the news.

I should talk a little bit about how the packing for the ride evolves as the ride goes on. It becomes more and more practical with each repack, and many times you learn things the hard way.

I mainly used the BCS, or Butt Compression System. I would take a packed plastic bag, sit on it, and roll my weight from one end to the other, pressing out all the air possible, and then zipping it shut. Of course one needs to be careful that there aren't sunglasses in the bag during compression, or beneath the main straps when strapping the main bag to the bike. Don't ask me how I know that.

The day was absolutely gorgeous, with a cloudless blue sky and the wind at our backs. Riding was like sitting in a hammock.

I also found it was important to either keep a few items in a bag to remember what it was for, or else label it with a marker, because all plastic bags look the same when they're empty, save for their size. Staying organized definitely saves time, and that's important when you're feeling rushed.

Wednesday, June 14
Deadwood, South Dakota, to Fairmont, Minnesota

4:00 a.m.: Up and out of bed
4:30 a.m.: Out of the room
4:45 a.m.: Pack the bike
5:00 a.m.: Coffee and a snack

5:30 a.m.: Morning briefing and prayer
6:00 a.m.: Kickstands up!

We all had the exact same expression of dread on our faces that morning as we packed our bikes, which would have been funny, if I had a sense of humor at that hour. However, I did notice that it wasn't as cold as had been predicted, a welcome and appreciated gift.

Becky had a special departing request for us. Many riders would film the group's departure on their last day, but this morning we were leaving from a parking garage, and you probably already guessed the request. She wanted to hear all the bikes start up at the same time, to record "The Song of Our People," as she often said, comically referring to the thundering sound of revving motorcycle engines. The group was only too happy to oblige, and besides, we really needed a morale raiser that morning.

We lined up in our usual way, and then silenced the bikes for a minute. On the signal, we hit those starters and revved our machines to life. The moment was exhilarating (and deafening), and Becky got it all on camera. We waved goodbye as we departed. Those moments were always a little bittersweet for me, as I knew with each departing member that my own day was getting closer, and that this great adventure was coming to an end.

Once out on the highway, we were met with another wonderful gift. The day was absolutely gorgeous, with a cloudless blue sky and the wind at our backs. Riding was like sitting in a hammock. I couldn't help but think that Mother Nature must have felt we had paid our dues and was rewarding us for our determination with incredible riding weather.

A funny thing about riding, it's not always the same every day. Some mornings I could get on the bike and wear it like a glove. Everything felt right, and I would throw my feet on the highway pegs and feel awesome and confident. Other days, nothing I could do could make me feel comfortable on the bike. Not the way I would sit in the seat, or place my feet on the footpads, or position my hands on the grips.

No matter how many times I would adjust, I just couldn't find that groove. And not feeling good on the bike meant uncertainty and stress, because it was just one more thing to have to deal with.

Many times I was thankful to have my CamelBak on, regardless of the temperature of the day. It not only kept me quenched during the long hours in the saddle, but it also kept me focused and alert at times. I had learned to recognize the feeling of drain, either physically or mentally, and would take a sip to refresh both. And once in awhile, it took my focus off the fear I felt while riding through the mountains. Did I mention I'm afraid of heights? I often thought it probably looked to cars passing by as if I was on some sort of oxygen, as it has a tendency under a helmet to look a bit Mad Max-ish.

At the first gas stop of the day, I was approached by a state trooper named Aric, who was very interested in our group.

Aric was probably in his late 30s, blonde and tall, and reminded me a little bit of the old television cartoon character Dudley Do-Right. He chatted me up as we both walked out of the gas station building.

"So where are you ladies headed?" he inquired.

"We're headed for Fairmont, Minnesota," I responded. "This is the Women's Freedom Ride, and we're doing 19 states in 18 days to raise money to provide service dogs for disabled veterans."

"Wow!" He replied. "That's amazing. How many of there are you?"

"About 30, I think," I said, "Riders fall in and out of the ride as we travel, joining us for a day or two, or whatever they can do."

"I always wanted a motorcycle," he said, "But my wife won't let me get one."

"Man, that's too bad," I told him. "Maybe you should get her a bike and she might change her mind!" I teased.

He came over to chat with the group, and even though the girls joked and gave him a hard time about being a cop, he took it in stride, so we gave him one of our posters and took a group photo with him. Afterward he gave us his number and told us to give him a call if we ran into any trouble on our way to Sioux Falls. What a great guy!

As we crossed South Dakota, I was amused by the silly things we saw along the roadside: a skeleton of a dinosaur and a giant sculpture of a bull peeking over a hill, to mention just a few. We enjoyed a simple lunch of hamburgers and hot dogs at the Harley-Davidson dealer in Sioux Falls, where I did a bit of yoga to ease my stiff lower back.

I found a cool place in the shade on the lush green grass next to the picnic tables and did a few minutes each of cat/cow, up dog, down dog, and ended with the bridge pose. It felt amazing to release the tension. I opened my eyes to see a lot of ladies glancing over, giving me odd looks. My workout seemed a little foreign to some of the ladies enjoying their lunch.

"You all right?" somebody inquired.

"That looks uncomfortable," said another.

I figured "biker" girls must do more riding than yoga. That's okay, we all have our priorities.

As the day wore on, it also grew very warm, and with the long miles for the day, the group began to show signs of wear and crabbiness. By the time we made it to our hotel in Fairmont, Minnesota, everyone was more than ready for the day to be over. Three women joining us that day from the Twin Cities/St. Croix area provided a lovely picnic-style meal in the hotel's breakfast area that evening. They were excited about the ride and wanted to do something special for us, which was very sweet.

Afterward I jumped in the shower to cool off and clean up, and spent the evening organizing my things, my thoughts, and my words, as tomorrow would be my return to home sweet home Wisconsin, and my last day on the road riding with the group.

Back to Wisconsin, Bike Night in Milwaukee, and Saying Goodbye

Thursday, June 15
Fairmont, Minnesota, to Milwaukee, Wisconsin

I mentioned earlier that my body would tell me in no uncertain terms how unhappy it was to be waking up at such early hours and asked to perform. Many mornings I would find myself in need of a bathroom, and right after the morning prayer, I'd have to hurry back into the hotel to find a ladies room.

It was this morning habit that made Ghost start saving her room keys. I didn't realize she'd been doing it, but there was a very close call at one of the hotels, and I guess that's when she started to save them, in order to save me.

It was 6:45 a.m. that morning when it hit. I looked at Ghost, and she simply held up a hand with hotel key cards spread across it like a poker hand. Feeling little sheepish, I grabbed the room key and hurried back to the room. I had 15 minutes, plenty of time.

Five minutes later I ran back out to my bike, only to find all the ladies lined up with their engines running. We never left early, so I was just a bit perturbed, but I grabbed my gear and jumped on my bike.

As I quickly cinched up the strap on my helmet, the guy in the van parked next to my bike chatted me up.

"Oh, no. Not now!" I thought.

"Hey there. What's all this about?" He asked.

I gave him the basic spiel about the ride as fast as I could without sounding rude. I kept my sentences very close together so he couldn't ask a lot of questions as I backed my bike out into the parking lot. The sound of 30-some Harley engines waiting to leave is not something to be taken lightly, even if they were all my friends at this point.

When I got to the end of my little promo speech, I told him I was sorry but "I really have to go, because all these ladies are waiting for ME!"

He nodded and waved me off as he wished us a safe ride. I rode over to my place in line and Momma put her thumb in the air. When all our thumbs were in the air, we were off!

The Ladies Refer To It As Dancin'

When a group of motorcyclists have been riding together for a time and things start to flow, that's dancin'. It's when you no longer count those two seconds between you and the next rider, you no longer struggle staying on your side of the lane, you don't actually think about where you need to be or how to react, you just know.

It's part of you now. You're no longer an individual, but part of a "murmuration." Similar to when a school of fish reacts as a single entity, the group is now a sum of its parts, a well-oiled machine, a dance. That's the state of mind I was in as we headed back to my home turf, Wisconsin. The night prior I had penned some of the words that I had played with in my head during the long miles on the road, trying to create a brief but complete goodbye to this amazing group of women I had been privileged to have become a part of.

It was an intense ride through rush hour traffic with merging lanes everywhere, and just when I figured we were in the clear, as we rounded the curve to South Milwaukee, there it was.

The time had come to figure it out and deliver it. We'd be staying in Milwaukee for two days, so there was still time to get it right. Heading east on I-90, which incidentally is the longest interstate highway in the United States, things started looking more and more familiar to me. As we neared the beautiful, rugged bluffs of La Crosse where I went to college, my heart began to race.

We headed down the slope to where I-90 crosses the mighty Mississippi, with me pumping my fist in the air and pointing to all the beauty of the valley, to show the pride I had for my home state. That pride was short lived, though, since Wisconsin roads were easily the worst we encountered on the trip. So bad, in fact, that some of the girls had damage to their bikes.

Still, everyone seemed in a playful mood when we stopped in Mauston for lunch. Momma Bear played a trick on the wait staff, and it was a good one. She used her straw to make a silly, strange sound, and since the source could not be located, the wait staff had an entertaining conversation about it. They gathered briefly with puzzled looks on their faces. It was hard to hear them amidst the noise of the diners, but I heard bits and pieces of their comments.

"What was that?"
"Not sure."
"Where did it come from?"
"I really don't know." (laughs)

As the staff continued to look around the dining room, trying to solve the mystery, a sly, amused Momma didn't let on, and we giggled at her cleverness. Surely such silliness could never have been generated by the leader of a "biker gang!" Unable to resolve the source of the sound, eventually the staff returned to their duties.

After lunch we broke into two groups to better navigate the Milwaukee traffic we were headed for. Ten minutes between the groups also meant an easier check-in at the hotel, which wouldn't be overwhelmed with almost two dozen women asking for room keys. The traffic and the wind became worse as we neared the big city. It was an intense ride through rush hour traffic with merging lanes everywhere, and just when I figured we were in the clear, as we rounded the curve to South Milwaukee, there it was.

Road construction across six lanes of traffic, looking like a demilitarized zone. As intimidating as it looked, I knew we couldn't be far from the hotel. I sucked up my dismay and sped on. My sister, Linda, filmed our arrival as we rolled in. I parked and got off my bike, and she walked up and gave me a long hug. It felt great, and I was glad to see her.

Linda was a big hit with the group, and joined us for dinner. She presented me with a trophy for completing the ride, stuffed with a little purple monkey adorned with a bandana and purple necklaces. Purple was the color for our ride, so it was significant. And now I had a riding buddy! According to his tag, his name was Grapes.

After supper we headed over to Bike Night at the Harley-Davidson Museum, and Linda was able to experience riding with us.

Bike Night is typically an evening sponsored by a dealership, inviting riders to come together and network, or just show off their bikes. You can imagine the large number of riders that this appeals to then, in a large metro area like Milwaukee.

My roommate Diane generously offered to take Linda along on the back of her trike. I wasn't sure if Linda would enjoy it, since during the evening runs we ride . . . shall we say . . . a little less "structured." I didn't know how she'd react to seeing her little sister tearing up downtown Milwaukee on her motorcycle.

I half expected a lecture about being more cautious, but to my surprise she was all about it and said it was a lot of fun! She asked how fast we had been going. I laughed and told her, "I never look at the speedometer, I just keep up!"

Having Linda along actually came in handy. Living so close to Milwaukee, she'd spent a lot of time there, and knew the streets well. Better than our navigation app, that is. The ride captains somehow took a wrong turn on the way from the hotel to the museum, and when they stopped to figure it out, Linda told them exactly which way to go.

Bike night turned out to be crowded, noisy, and full of posers (in my opinion), so we didn't stay much more than an hour. We grabbed a bite to eat, strolled through the shop for a few minutes, made our way back to the bikes, and then decided to head back to the hotel. I don't think I have ever seen so many bikes in one place, though.

Back at the hotel, Linda offered to take my laundry home, and having nothing left to prove, I let her. She really seemed to enjoy her time with the ladies of the ride, and I was glad she had a chance to meet and spend some time with them.

Friday, June 16, was a layover day in Milwaukee, so while many were off touring the local museums, I took time to do a little shopping, as our hotel was right next to a motorcycle shop that for once wasn't a Harley dealership. Elated at the thought, I headed over to check out jackets, helmets, and a few other items. After two weeks on a motorcycle, you have a very clear idea of what you want, and I had a wish list.

I ended up purchasing a ram mount for my bike and installed it myself that afternoon. A ram mount is a device that quickly adjusts on the spot to hold items like a cell phone or other similarly shaped article. This comes in handy when you need to navigate in an area you are unfamiliar with, since your hands are busy shifting, braking, and accelerating. You can have a navigating app open on your phone and refer to it safely and easily. When not using my phone, it makes a nice spot for my stuffed monkey Grapes, since the mount has additional rubber bungee-like loops to ensure you don't lose your device when the road gets rough. I easily wrap the loops around his appendages and he smiles at me as I roll down the road.

Ghost was still having problems with her bike and had rolled it over to the shop to have it evaluated. The part she needed wouldn't be available until Monday, and she'd be back home by then. To make things worse, her battery was dead and the bike wouldn't even start, so Ghost rode the bike, while Jean, one of the ride captains, and I pushed, so we could pop the clutch to get it running, to get it back to the trailer.

After supper, there was a brief meeting about the next day's ride to Indiana. The concern was road construction but also the weather. Once again Linda made some good suggestions to the road captains about good routes to take that would avoid the road construction and still help them make good time, so they could beat the rain that was on the way.

After running to get gas for the bike, I returned to the lobby to find Linda still saying goodbye to the group. I thought it was neat that she bonded with the girls in such a short time and glad that she enjoyed herself.

Most of the ladies retired early, as the following morning would bring one of the earliest departures of the ride. Back at the room, I organized as many of my things as I could before bed, took a shower, and turned in.

Saturday, June 17
Last Day of My Ride

The room was up at 3:30 a.m. with our usual routine. I am typically the last one out of the room, and this morning was no different. I was thankful this time, though, because as I was strapping on my half chaps, tears welled up in my eyes. It wasn't the first time this had happened. A few times during the last week, I had thought about my last day and tears had come then, too. But I needed to focus on the road and traffic, so I pushed it all out of my mind.

I was fine until I looked at Ghost's face. Then I lost it.

How is it that these women who were strangers two weeks ago have come to be so special to me in such a short time? Through an odyssey of highs and lows, fun times and danger, and sharing laughter, gifts, advice, and deep emotions, I had come to know them much more deeply and differently than I did that wet afternoon they rolled into the hotel parking lot in Paducah.

The hotel staff knew we were leaving extra early and set up a simple breakfast to accommodate us, which everyone deeply appreciated. I was fine until I looked at Ghost's face. Then I lost it. Karen and I had grown very close very quickly during the ride. We found we had a lot in common. She had taken me under her wing and made sure I was on time, had the right stuff on, and teased me when I fussed too much. She listened to my ranting when I was frustrated and mercilessly gave me shit when I was "too" anything. In short, she took a really tough job and did it magnificently.

The time came for the group to depart. Before the prayer was read, I asked to say a few words. Momma got the group's attention, and gave me the floor. Holding back tears, I managed to read through the rough notes I had made a few nights prior:

"I just want to thank everyone for letting me be a part of this ride. Thank you for your friendship, all your tips, your gifts, and your advice. I appreciate it. Thanks especially to Ghost for keeping an eye on me. It's not an easy job looking after me . . . she did a great job, and she needs a raise! My goal on this ride was to get through it without doing something stupid to get myself or anyone else killed *(to which the ladies responded with wild hoots and applause, and I smiled through my tears),* and I'm glad to say I met my goal. And with that, I'd like to present this check to Momma."

Then I handed my donation check over to Momma—Karen Collins, the organizer of the ride, a woman with a lot of love in her heart. She gave me a big hug and whispered some lovely things to me as she held me, one of which was that she was glad I had come along on the ride. A simple thought, but it meant everything to me.

As the bikes lined up, I positioned myself to video the final departure. The ladies waved as they passed by, one by one. At the end of the line was Ghost, riding in the chase vehicle once again. She waved and shouted out the window, "Love you, girl!" and I hollered, "Love you!" right back.

I watched until they were out of sight, and waited until I could no longer hear the mighty roar of their engines. I quietly walked back to my bike, and after shedding a few more tears, Xena and I pulled out of the parking lot a few minutes after.

I took back roads all the way back home, savoring the last moments of my adventure. It was a four-hour ride, but it passed like it was no time at all. I pulled into my driveway about 9:30 a.m., feeling an incredible sense of accomplishment and pride. I pulled off my helmet, and gave my dog a very, very long hug.

Epilogue: All Good Things Must Come to an End . . . or Must They?

Wow, what a great adventure, and I, too, am a little sad that it's over. I am so happy to have been able to share it with you. The idea, the preparation, the anticipation, the agony and the ecstasy.

What happened in the weeks that followed my return? Well, I have to say it was difficult assimilating back into "normal" life. Our morning meetings on the ride always began with basic information. What number day of the ride it was, what date on the calendar it was, and what day of the week it was "in the real world," as Tink would always say.

We actually used that phrase, because after so many days on the road, it all became a blur, and we knew we were no longer part of what most people would refer to as normal. No, waking up before dawn to ride 300 to 400 miles each day at 80 mph with a group of women on motorcycles is definitely not normal.

Many times it was hard to remember where we were, what time zone we were in, and where we were headed. You get used to pulling into to a strange place, seeing people pull out their cameras, and getting interviewed by people brave enough to approach. There's a rhythm to it, and once it's gone, you have to regain your sense of purpose and adjust.

I have to be honest . . . going to the grocery store is a bit mundane after you've done a two-week stint as a rock star. "Really? I'm buying a head of cauliflower?" I took a long time to unpack, because I just didn't want it all to be over. I was very sad to reach the bottom of the duffel and see it empty. I was also shocked to count upwards of 70 plastic bags used. Yes, I counted them.

Other interesting stats: 12 states in 16 days. An estimated 64 gas stops. Tank capacity: 4.41 gallons. Miles per tank: 180 before using the reserve, which allows roughly 40 more miles, but don't trust it. Bike weight with oil and gas: 613 lbs. Maximum load: 463 lbs. (I didn't weigh my pack, but I doubt it threatened the maximum load for the bike at any point, even after subtracting my weight from it.)

I've also taken to doing very long rides on the weekend because I miss those hours on the road. I really do. But it's strange to be riding all alone down the highway and not with 30 other bikes. Confidence? It's through the roof. I should come with a warning label now. After two weeks of facing extreme heat and cold, brutal winds, driving rain, ugly stares, rude remarks, and deep doubt and continuing on in spite of intense physical and mental fatigue, there's no longer anything to fear. Once you are pushed beyond your limits, you realize everything you're capable of.

Now what I thought was heavy wind before, barely registers on my radar. Having ridden in a literally blinding rainstorm, I have a whole new threshold on riding in the rain. Passing semi trucks used to terrify me when I set out on this ride, but now, it's more like, "Semi? What semi?" It's kind of the perspective you have on pain after having experienced childbirth.

Many have asked if I would do or will do the ride again. I was flattered to have been asked to join 2018's ride before our ride was over, and took that as a great compliment. I was also asked to join the group the weekend they plan next year's ride, another lovely request from my new riding buddies. As Sally Field would say, "They like me! They really, really like me!"

Unfortunately, planning weekend is held at the end of October, at the Ironhorse Lodge in Robbinsville, North Carolina, and that's a long way to ride by myself during a time of year when the weather is fickle, and I can't afford to fly in, although there were offers to pick me up at the airport if I did, two hours away. And though I will miss four days of fun riding with my "Wind Sisters" in the mountains of North Carolina, my heart will be with them.

The answer to the question of whether I'll do the ride again depends on a lot of variables: where the ride will go next year, how far I have to travel to join up with the group, what kind of vacation time I have available, and, of course, the funds I have at the time. I used my own vacation time and my own funds to pay for my expenses. All the donations were just that, and sent on to the cause, except for one or two very rare exceptions, where I was given a choice by some sweet donors.

So what's next, you ask? Do I have any plans for future adventures?

Hell, yeah! Or as my big sister Linda put it, "How do we keep you in the yard now?"

Indeed.

Appendix:

Bike Stats

2010 Yamaha 950 V-Star:
Gas Mileage: 47 mpg
Tank Capacity: 4.41 gallons
Weight with oil & gas: 613#
Max Load: 463#

Appendix:

GoFundMe Letter

Hi everyone,

I've got some big plans for June. I've joined the Women's Freedom Ride 2017!

The Women's Freedom Ride is an amazing all female cross country motorcycle ride, supporting, encouraging, and raising awareness of women riders. In 2017, the Women's Freedom Ride will be traveling through 19 states and over 6000 miles, with hundreds of women coming together to join in on this amazing journey.

The ride runs June 3-20, and begins in Charleston, SC and ends in Statesville, NC. I will be joining the ride from their stop in Paducah, KY on June 4 until they head out for Indianapolis from Milwaukee on June 17th. We'll spend two weeks riding through Illinois, Missouri, Kansas, Colorado, Wyoming, Idaho, Montana, South Dakota, Minnesota, and Wisconsin. I hope to write about it (already started), and do a few Live Facebook videos during our stops on the route to promote the charity. Since the longest I've ever spent on my motorcycle has been about three hours, it should be a very interesting and challenging experience for me.

The Women's Freedom Ride also believes in supporting our country's Veterans. Each year they choose a veteran-related charity, and 100% of the donations raised will be given to that charity. Each rider covers her own expenses on the ride.

This year, our chosen charity is the Patriot Rovers. Patriot Rovers is a 501c3 organization that trains and provides service dogs for Veterans. These amazing animals provide assistance with everyday activities, from getting help, turning lights off and on, opening doors, dressing, and all standard service dog tasks. One of the most wonderful things about these dogs is the unconditional love and companionship they provide. The group is hoping to raise $21,000 for the training of service dogs for three disabled veterans.

I would like to take this opportunity to invite you to participate in this year's event by donating to our cause, or perhaps becoming a sponsor. Your generosity would make a huge difference in the life of a Veteran!

If you'd like to sponsor the ride as a business, Please contact me personally for the details. If you'd like to learn more about the ride, please go to womensfreedomride.org.

Thanks for taking the time to read this and considering supporting our cause. I'm really looking forward to this adventure!

~ Paula

Appendix:

Packing Suggestions

Women's Freedom Ride Packing Suggestions
CamelBak
Sunscreen
Bug Spray
Lip Balm
Meds for muscles aches, allergies, etc.
Boots, Tennis Shoes, Flip Flops
Jeans (3) wear one
Tee Shirts (3) buy some as souvenirs
Tank Tops (2)
Long-Sleeve Shirts (1) Drywick
Sweatshirt
Hoodie/Jacket
PJ's
Casual clothes (shorts, yoga pants)
Underwear (5) Drywick or boxers
Socks (3)
Ziploc bags (all sizes)
Trash Bags
Zip Ties
Bungees/ROC Straps
Net strap
Octane Booster

Tool Kit
Face covers/Bandannas
Leathers/Gloves
Rain Suit
Bathing Suit
Cooling Vest
Sunglasses/yellow-lensed glasses
Band-Aids
Phone/Charger
Insurance
Pen
Registration
Protein Snacks
Toothpaste, Toothbrush
Shampoo/Conditioner
Soap, Deodorant
Razor
Nail Clippers
Tweezers
Lotion
Laundry Detergent Pods

Gary's Packing List
Motorcycle:
Air Hawk Seat
Duffel Bag
Plastic Bag Liner (big orange Fleet Farm one)
Extra Ziploc Bags
2 sets of Cycle Keys
Flashlights/Batteries

Bungee Cords & Net
Tools
Maps
Rainsuit/Boot Covers
Ear Plugs
Notepad & Pen
Reservation form for hotel
Can Cooler
Wallet, Money, Credit Card
Cell Phone/Charger
Digital Camera
Sunscreen
Sunglasses, Clear riding glasses
Knife, Leatherman
Cycle lock & key
Bike rags
Lighter

Clothing:
Leather jacket
Leather vest
Baseball cap
Gloves & Fingerless
Bandannas
Boots, sandals, tennis shoes
Jeans (3)
Sweatshirt
Shorts
Swimsuit
Tee shirts

Long-sleeved tees
Underwear
Socks
Pajamas
Bag for dirty clothes

Toiletries:
Pills
Aspirin and others
Toothpaste, toothbrush
Chapstick
Eyeglasses
Contacts & solution
Deodorant
Bar of soap
Shampoo
Towel & washcloth
Handkerchiefs
Comb & folding brush, mirror
Shave cream & shaver
Antibiotic Cream
Floss
Q-tips
Eye drops
Cough drops
Chewing gum
Antacids
First Aid Kit
Reading glasses
License

Bike Registration
Proof of Insurance

Author's Packing List
Layers:
Tank
Short-Sleeve Tee
Long-Sleeve Tee
Light Jacket
Leather Jacket
Under Armour
Leggings
Baggy Jeans
Warm socks

Wearing:
Half chaps
1 pair of gloves
Angel pin
Boots
Watch
1 pair jeans
Compression socks
Compression sleeves
Neck gaiter/tube
Helmet, Jacket, Ear Plugs
CamelBak

Tan Backpack:
Dry bag

Safety pins
Meds
Eye drops
Snacks
Monkey Butt Powder
Desitin/Vagisil
Poise
License
Registration
Insurance
Toilet bag
Laundry detergent pods
Soap

Black Backpack:
Full chaps
2nd set of keys
Extra bags
Jacket liner
Leatherman
2nd neck gaiter

Quick Access Pockets of Duffel Bag:
Rain Poncho
Rain Gear
All gloves
Baseball cap
2 sunglasses
Bandannas
First Aid Kit

Fleece jacket
Hoodie
Wipes
Protein Snacks

Fork Bag behind windshield (Quickest Access):
Wallet, credit card
Knife
Pepper spray
Fingerless gloves
Chapstick
Phone
Sunscreen
Pen & paper
Camera
Ear plugs

Saddlebag - right (inside):
Extra bungees
Carabiners
Flashlight
Headlamp

Saddlebag - left (outside):
Extra tie-downs
Novus windshield cleaner
Bug spray

Main Section of Duffel Bag:
All clothes

Towel
Kitchen garbage bags for laundry
Handkerchiefs
All shoes
All chargers, tablet, power strip

Appendix:

Women's Freedom Ride 2017 Stops at a Glance

Saturday, June 3: Charleston, South Carolina, to Knoxville, Tennessee
Sunday, June 4: Knoxville, Tennessee, to Paducah, Kentucky
Monday, June 5: Paducah, Kentucky, to Blue Springs, Missouri
Tuesday, June 6: Blue Springs, Missouri, to Hays, Kansas
Wednesday, June 7: Hays, Kansas, to Fort Collins, Colorado
Thursday, June 8: Fort Collins, Colorado, to Rock Springs, Wyoming
Friday, June 9: Rock Springs, Wyoming, to Idaho Falls, Idaho
Saturday, June 10: Idaho Falls (layover)
Sunday June 11: Idaho Falls, Idaho, to Billings, Montana
Monday, June 12: Billings, Montana, to Deadwood, South Dakota
Tuesday, June 13: Deadwood (layover)
Wednesday, June 14: Deadwood, South Dakota, to Fairmont, Minnesota
Thursday, June 15: Fairmont, Minnesota, to Milwaukee, Wisconsin
Friday, June 16: Milwaukee, Wisconsin (layover)
Saturday, June 17: Milwaukee, Wisconsin to Indianapolis, Indiana
Sunday June 18: Indianapolis, Indiana, to Marietta, Ohio
Monday, June 19: Marietta, Ohio, to Statesville, North Carolina

For more information about the Women's Freedom Ride, visit
www.womensfreedomride.org

More from Paula . . .

To read more of Paula's writing, visit *ladylovinherlife.com*

Coming soon!

Up next from Paula O'Kray:
Lady Lovin' Her Life, a compilation of Paula's popular published columns from "Middle of the Road" in the *Portage County Gazette.*

Paula O'Kray is a graphic designer, columnist, and Wisconsin native. Mother of two and grandmother of four, Paula lives in central Wisconsin with her fuzzy half lab, half chow Ms. K and spends her time considering new and interesting adventures that will continue to pull her out of her comfort zone.

www.ingramcontent.com/pod-product-compliance
Lightning Source LLC
Chambersburg PA
CBHW050816090426
42736CB00022B/3474